The Illustrated Step·by·Step Chinese Cookbook

by Paul C. Huang

ILLUSTRATED BY GARY COOLEY

AND LANCE GERSHENOFF

SIMON AND SCHUSTER   NEW YORK

to my daughter Pamela Mei-ling

Published by Simon and Schuster
Rockefeller Center, 630 Fifth Avenue
New York, New York 10020

Manufactured in the United States of America

1 2 3 4 5 6 7 8 9 10

Library of Congress Cataloging in Publication Data
Huang, Paul C.
   The illustrated step-by-step Chinese cookbook.
   1. Cookery, Chinese. I. Title.
TX724.5.C5H79   641.5'951   75-9536
ISBN 0-671-22103-5

CONTENTS

INTRODUCTION

In the 1940s, I traveled up the Tung River in southern China on a huge salt-laden junk. I remember we stopped at the foot of a gorge for the night before attempting to pass through the rapids. The sky was a bright, light blue, with the hilltops on either side of the river crowned by the golden light of the setting sun. And down by the riverbanks, dusk was rising slowly, making the ground a shadowless gray—and cool to the bottoms of my bare feet. The shoreline was dangerously rocky, paralleled by a smooth, well-worn, narrow footpath.

The Tung River is like the history of China: there are periods of calm and periods of great turbulence. Traveling up the river in a cargo junk sort of summarizes life there: you can pole the junk up river with a crew of six in the gentle, glassy waters, but you'd need the help of a hundred strong-backed men to inch her through the rapids.

This struggle between nature and life, the contrast between violence and serenity (within sight of each other) seems most natural because we've come to accept it. And its acceptance is reflected in our lives and art.

I had never met any river coolies before, and I didn't know quite what to expect. Being a curious little boy and somewhat bored with the narrow confines of junk life, I decided to explore the shoreline.

They were dressed in either black or gray pants, rolled up to the knees. A few had gray shirts draped over their backs, but most of them were still bare-chested and hot from the day's work. The last boat of the day had passed through their gorge, and now they sat on the heels of their feet, a huge bowl of rice in one hand and chopsticks in the other. The men sat in a perfect circle around a pot of fish with brown gravy, a large dish of pork with vegetables, a steaming bowl of soup and a wooden bucket of rice. They ate with gusto and a lot of loud chatter. Now and then one or two of them would reach in to replenish their rice bowls with more vegetables, or fish, or both. They worked their chopsticks like miniature shovels, pushing and scooping the food around the bowl and into their mouths. And the sounds of their eating carried the spirit of life and fellowship. I always had the feeling that the noise they made while eating was in tribute to the cook and to give thanks; that they purposely ate by the riverside to let the river and the rocks know that they had seen the passing of another day . . . without the loss of life. The evening meal was a celebration. And when one of them spotted me standing

there, staring at them, they invited me to sit and share their meal.

Several years later, in Shanghai, after World War II, an uncle treated me to a Sunday brunch—just the two of us, separated by a round, white marble table. It was a warm spring day and a soft breeze danced its way between the green columns of the gazebo.

Tea was served first in a glazed green teapot—and green cups—both designed to match the green tiles of the gazebo roof. Then the servants proceeded to serve dumplings, or *dim sem,* in white porcelain plates—naturally, they matched the white marble table and floor. There were thirty varieties of dumplings, three to a plate. It took the chef and his three helpers all morning to prepare the brunch. Both the food and the setting were perfect. Confucius couldn't have asked for better.

Food has always been an important part of life. A lot of thought goes into the preparation and serving of it. After all, isn't eating a celebration of life?

Anyone who grows up in China or takes the time to learn about the Chinese cuisine will realize that it is an art form within a social setting—an art form that is understood by everyone and practiced daily . . . full of symbolism and humanity.

When my father takes the family out to dinner, there is always a discussion between him and the waiter in the restaurant. If it's an occasion, say a birthday, he'll tell the waiter that and ask him to recommend the chef's best noodle dish. (You always order at least one noodle dish on a birthday because the long, uncut noodle is a symbol of longevity.) Since there are at least several hundred different noodle dishes, this discussion may take some time. There are two reasons for the discussion: First, by not immediately accepting the waiter's suggestions and by countering with a number of your own, you've effectively told the chef that this is an important occasion and you'll go to some lengths to make things just right—but you've said it without actually saying it. Second, because there are so many dishes in the Chinese cuisine (I would guess that only about 5 to 10 percent of them are listed in a restaurant's menu) you do yourself and the chef great honor if you pick a dish that's seldom called for, especially if that dish taxes the chef's creativity. And the appreciation is mutual.

I've seen occasions where the chef came out to congratulate *my father* for ordering a flawless meal—and in return, being congratulated for preparing it to perfection. It's a unique form of stroking.

In old China, where most people farmed the land, big families were an asset. Today, China favors small families, but family life has not changed. From the time you are old enough to work in the fields and help do the chores around the house, you are a valued member of the family. You become an integral member of a close knit, social-economic unit. You produce.

Most Chinese become fairly accomplished at wrapping dumplings and sealing spring rolls at an early age. Most of us could do rather well by the time we were eight. We could do it without any help or coaching from mother or grandmother. And we took great pride in achieving the complex multiple folds that only deft fingers could execute. The acquisition of such skills tended to enhance your position in the family—it was proof that you had made it, and that's a good feeling.

Every Sunday morning, as was the custom with most northern Chinese families, we all sat around the table preparing the midday meal. The preparations were well orchestrated, the sounds and motions were rhythmic and flowing, and they could be heard throughout the house. There was the steady rat-a-tat-tat of a cleaver dicing pork, the intermittent tat-ta-tat-tat of dicing scallions, and the crunch, crunch of the cleaver cutting through heads of Chinese cabbage. Occasionally there would be the SLAP of a roll of dough smashed against the table top. Underneath these sounds was the constant chatter of high-pitched voices, gossiping, pleading, ordering, laughing. The sounds of a family at work and at play. A satisfying, full sound.

And while the women and children were thus occupied, the men attended to the outdoor chores, like feeding the chickens and pigs. When finished, the men would sit in the sunshine smoking their long pipes and listening to the opera that flowed out of the kitchen, their faces reflecting tranquility and contentment. The men in the family were being honored for their week's toil in the fields. The family was one because everyone understood his duties. Giv-

ing to the family wasn't so much an act of selflessness as one of tradition. It was a part of life that no one questioned. There were no conflicts.

To experience that feeling of family on a warm spring day is what life is all about. That feeling permeated the house through the kitchen, defined the family, and nurtured the individual happiness of each member.

Preparation, cooking, and eating is a celebration that the entire family participates in. No one is excluded, and that's what makes it fun.

Most of the work in making Chinese food is the preparation. And one way to take the tedium out of it is to enlist the help of your family and friends. Give each person a job to do, and you'll see how fast the work gets done. The noise, the chatter, the action, and the knowledge of the fact that you are doing something together and for each other will make it more than worthwhile. And the food will taste better to everyone, too! Who's going to criticize his own handiwork, no matter how little?

how to use this book

To cook Chinese food is fast and easy. The art is in the preparation. Can you slice pork into wafer-thin strips? And cut vegetables into uniform sections? How well you do this plays a significant part in the way your dishes will turn out.

Most dishes are cooked by the stir-cooking method. The basic idea is to keep the ingredients in the frying pan in constant motion. The sliced meats and cut vegetables will then be exposed to the heat evenly—which means that they will all be cooked at the same time. If you don't keep the food in motion, then the bottom layer will get cooked first, and you'll have a good chance of burning some of it.

The major benefit of this method is that the meat and vegetables cook quickly so that the natural juices are locked in by the searing action of the hot oil.

Almost every dish is cooked with either vegetable oil or peanut oil. The hot oil helps to cook the ingredients, keep them from sticking to the bottom of the pan (getting burned), and, most important, it gently coats the food to lock in the natural juices and flavor.

Because of this method, here's what you have to keep in mind when you use this book: There are no absolutes in this book (except this sentence). By that I mean, don't follow my cooking time too closely. The cooking times are calculated from my stove and by the way I slice the meats and vegetables. First, I never slice the meat the same thickness every time I cook. If I'm in a hurry, I slice it a little thicker, and if I'm entertaining and I've allocated enough time to the task, then I slice the meat finer. All you need to do is slice it a fraction of an inch thinner to lessen the cooking time.

Second, different stoves put out different amounts of heat. I cook everything on a gas stove. (So beware, you electric-stove owners, because I have had no experience with electric stoves or what effect they have on this type of cooking. I can imagine that you'll have some problems because you can't reduce the heat quickly enough. The coils just won't go out instantly. One way around that is to lift the frying pan off the heat and rest it on an unused burner.) But different gas stoves behave differently, too. The gas jets are not uniform in size, hence the amount of heat output will affect the cooking time for every dish. I found this out the hard way because I've moved several times in the course of preparing this book. And the stoves have all been different, and the cooking times have varied from stove to stove.

As you can see, there are a number of variables to contend with: how thinly and evenly you slice things, and the amount of heat your stove puts out.

You can overcome these minor inconsistencies by experimentation, by tasting the food as you cook it, and by looking for these things:

1. Don't let the meat, any kind of meat, get wrinkled-looking, limp, or dry. If you don't trust your eyes, just take out a piece and bite into it.
2. The same is true of vegetables—don't let them get shriveled up. Don't cook the juice out of them. Keep them green and firm. When you bite into a piece of vegetable, it should crunch.
3. Use my time as a general guide—don't be afraid to exceed it or reduce it. Experimentation and experience will be your best guide. Besides, Chinese cooking is creative, and part of the creativity is to develop your own sense of judgment, timing, and the amount of ingredients for each dish. Things are happening too fast for you to be concerned with the cooking steps and the sweep of a second hand. I haven't yet met a great chef who cooks by the clock!

Other variables to be aware of are spices and soy sauce. Each brand has slightly different qualities. For example, the different brands of soy sauce vary because they are made in slightly different ways. Some are saltier than others, and some are more flavorful than others. The best thing to do is find a brand you like, use my recipe as a general guide, but adjust the amount of soy sauce according to your choice of brand. The same is true for curry powder, ground ginger, and other spices. Different brands have different strengths.

Being creative isn't easy; it takes a little work.

Cooking is an art form that one practices daily. So you can imagine my frustration when I was transferred to White Sands Proving Grounds, New Mexico, where there was no Chinatown nearby, and no Chinese ingredients. The late fifties and early sixties were the days of great technological challenge on the one hand, and culinary on the other. I was determined to cook Chinese food for myself and friends in the wilds of the desert. But how? I improvised. I would only cook dishes with ingredients that the local supermarket supplied.

This is the result—an authentic Chinese Cookbook that you can use no matter where you live.

Since I learned the basics from watching my mother and grandmother prepare and cook Chinese food, I think it's only fair that you get the benefit of "watching" how it's done. And for that reason, we've taken the time and effort to give you illustrations which are commensurate with the celebrations of life.

HOW TO HOLD YOUR CHOPSTICKS

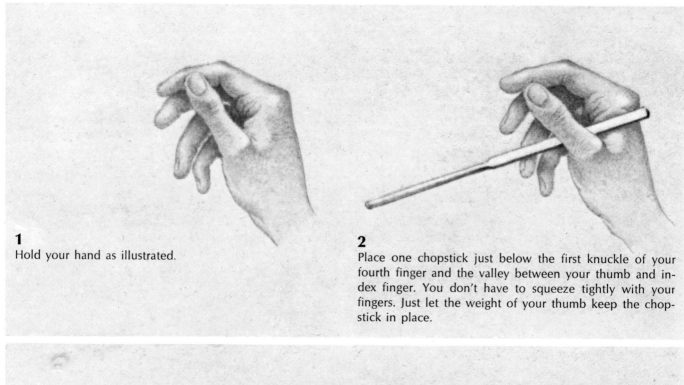

1
Hold your hand as illustrated.

2
Place one chopstick just below the first knuckle of your fourth finger and the valley between your thumb and index finger. You don't have to squeeze tightly with your fingers. Just let the weight of your thumb keep the chopstick in place.

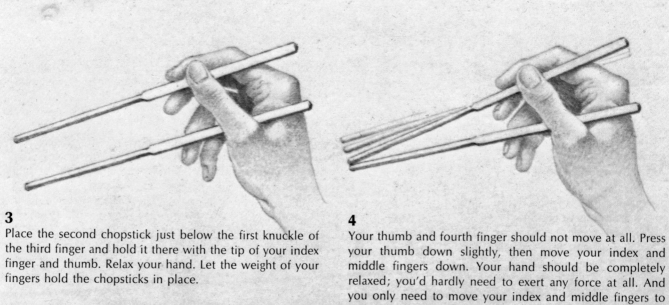

3
Place the second chopstick just below the first knuckle of the third finger and hold it there with the tip of your index finger and thumb. Relax your hand. Let the weight of your fingers hold the chopsticks in place.

4
Your thumb and fourth finger should not move at all. Press your thumb down slightly, then move your index and middle fingers down. Your hand should be completely relaxed; you'd hardly need to exert any force at all. And you only need to move your index and middle fingers to make your chopsticks work.

HOW TO COOK RICE

ingredients

1 cup long-grain rice (serves 2)
1 cup cold water

Total prep & cooking time: 20 minutes

Some rice packages tell you not to wash rice because it washes away nutrients, but I find that rice is often not clean. If you choose not to wash it, you may see a film of grime on top after cooking.

to prepare

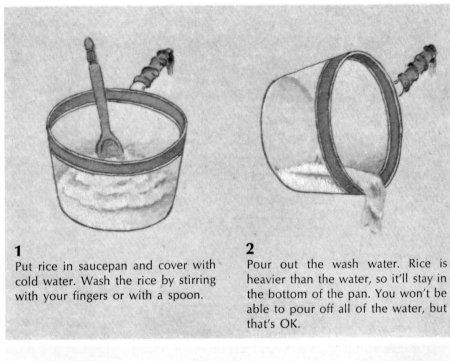

1
Put rice in saucepan and cover with cold water. Wash the rice by stirring with your fingers or with a spoon.

2
Pour out the wash water. Rice is heavier than the water, so it'll stay in the bottom of the pan. You won't be able to pour off all of the water, but that's OK.

to cook

1
Add 1 cup water to 1 cup rice after washing. In general, the amount of water should be the same as the amount of rice you want to cook.

2
Turn on a high flame. Bring the rice to a rapid boil with the pan uncovered.

3
When the water begins to boil rapidly, reduce the flame to low and cover the pan.

4
Cook the rice over low heat for 20 minutes. Don't stir it and don't remove the cover because you'll lose some of the steam pressure. Serve unseasoned.

MENU PLANNING

Classical Chinese literature is full of descriptions of famous feasts commissioned by kings and emperors. Chefs and spices were imported for the occasion and the menu planned with exquisite care. There were philosophical discussions about the placement of the fish (the fish is always served whole, and its head always pointed at the guest of honor. You'll see why in the fish section). What if there were two guests of equal rank? Then two fish would be chosen, but they must not be prepared the same way. Then the host would agonize further over the fish: Would the flavor of one conflict with the flavor of the other? And would the rest of the feast conflict with the subtle flavors of the fish? Should there be a hot Szechuan dish, and would the spiciness of the dish conflict with the tastes of all the other dishes? Perhaps a mild soup should be served after the hot dish to wash the palate clear for the tastes that follow? Should it be a green vegetable soup or a white vegetable soup? Which color works best with this meal?

Affairs of state were carefully planned, and the populace received descriptions of each feast. The public could judge the importance of the affair by the dishes served, and one could easily see the fortunes of the guests come or go depending on the symbolism of the meal. Scholars would compare the menus of this feast with some classical feasts: Did this one come up to par? How grave was the insult? How sublime the praise? Such was the matter of classical literature. And such is the tradition of the Chinese cuisine.

There are six ways to plan a menu. And the variations among the six make up the complicated procedure followed by cognoscenti—both for planning their own menus, and for ordering in a restaurant. The basic rules of thumb are these:

1. Pick a dish from each food category: a pork dish, a poultry dish, a beef, seafood, and vegetable. That's for a family of five or six people. But more on that later.
2. Pick combinations of dishes by their colors.
3. Pick dishes by their various tastes.
4. Pick dishes by the seasons (what's fresh for any growing season).
5. Balance dishes between meat and vegetables.
6. And remember that rice and soup are always an integral part of any Chinese meal.

1. Picking a dish from each category is the easiest thing to do when you have six people for dinner. But what do you do when you have two people? Just pick two dishes and a soup—but one of the two dishes should have a vegetable in it. For example: Drunken Chicken and Beef with Asparagus; or Roast Pork and Chicken with Asparagus. That's during the asparagus season, when asparagus is fresh and reasonable in price. This is where the seasonal aspect of menu planning comes into play.

For three people, a good thing to do is to have one seafood dish and two meat dishes with vegetables. For example: White Water Fish or Lobster Cantonese (or any seafood without vegetables in it), Ground Pork with String Beans and Shredded Chicken with Green Peas.

For four people, pick a stew or a big dish like Red-Cooked Pork, a seafood with vegetable like Shrimp with Peas, a Beef with Scallions, and a Chicken with Hot Pepper Sauce.

The reason I haven't mentioned a menu for five people is that the menu for six is usually about right for five, with a little bit left over—so five and six can be the same. For more than six people, you add one dish for each additional person. And the general rule is one dish per person attending the dinner, plus soup and rice.

You should only plan on serving hot (spicy) dishes when there are four people or more for dinner. The reason is this: with three other dishes plus soup and rice, the hotness of the dish won't be as overbearing. The flavors from the other dishes will temper and tone the heat. This is another good reason to serve a large bowl of hot soup with dinner. The hot soup will help wash the hot spices away, preparing your palate for the other dishes. I am assuming that you are serving your meal "family style," that is all the dishes are served at the same time. At banquets dishes are served one at a time, from the most elaborate to the simplest. The reason for that order is that you can eat your fill of the best dishes and not feel "left out" of the simpler or plain dishes that come last. And if you are planning a banquet for six of your favorite people, start with a duck, Chicken Velvet, Barbecued Beef, any seafood dish, Pork with Hot Peppers, Szechuan Style, and end up with Sweet-and-Sour Cabbage, and Watercress Soup or Cucumber Soup.

2. Planning by color. Obviously, you can't plan a menu by

color unless you already know most of the dishes, or you already know what color they are (and that's why we have color illustrations). But there are ways to figure out what the colors might be before you cook them. For example, lobsters will be red, and shrimps will be slightly pink. Any dish that has a lot of soy sauce in it (by a lot I mean more than three tablespoons) will turn out brown, dark brown, or reddish brown. Any dish that has a lot of soy sauce *and* a lot of dry sherry will be a sort of reddish brown, especially if it is pork. Vegetables are green, except Chinese cabbage, which is more white than green when cut the Chinese way. Any dish with catsup in it will turn out red. (I've used catsup in this book because it's less wasteful than using a few tablespoons of tomato paste and having so much of it left over. When I used to use tomato paste, I would walk around feeling bad   if I didn't use it up.)

Food is always more appetizing if the colors are right. So, whether you are planning a menu for two or for six, work up a good color scheme. It's very pleasing to the eye to see red, green, white, and light brown set in some combination on the table. (It would not be a good idea to set a table with four brown dishes.) This general idea should be followed when ordering in restaurants. Order with color in mind, because that's how Chinese food is prepared. Ingredients are arranged in colorful arrays, even within one dish, like pineapple fish: brown and white with golden nuggets of pineapple.

Just imagine a table set in red, gold, green, brown, and white: the red from lobster or any dish with catsup in it; the color of a golden sunset from curry, like curried chicken; the green from peas, asparagus, or green beans; the brown from a whole fish, and the white from soup and rice. So, consider color when you plan your menu.

3. Planning by taste. The only thing you have to worry about is this: Don't plan a menu that has conflicting tastes in it—or one with too many of the same tastes in it. For example, one hot, spicy dish in a meal is enough; even then, that dish should be chosen when you have four or more people to feed. The same is true of sweet-and-sour dishes, as much as you may like them. The taste is too overbearing if there are just two or three of you eating. It's much more pleasant to have sweet-and-sour dishes when you have lots of other tastes around to counterbalance the sweet flavoring; otherwise it's like eating dessert with the main course. In China it is unusual to plan a meal for two or three people. In fact, it's difficult to do because the food was designed for large families. It would be a disaster to have, say, White Water Fish and Sweet-and-Sour Pork! That would be comparable to eating hot apple pie *with,* not after, fillet of sole—you'd kill the delicate taste of the fish. And the point of planning a Chinese menu is harmony. Just make sure that the tastes work with each other, that they blend from one to the other, that there are dishes to counteract other dishes, like a good soup to offset any hot, spicy dish. Or a heavy brown sauce, like any red-cooked meat, to offset the sweet-and-sour dishes. If you balance out the strong flavors, you'll be able to enjoy the subtle flavors better. And you can only do this with the Chinese cuisine. No other cuisine gives you the variety of tastes within the same meal. That's the uniqueness of Chinese cooking.

Planning by taste is easy. Just do what comes naturally. If any combination offends you, remember not to repeat that combination again. The harmony of tastes has to be learned, and it's different for everyone. If you are the host, just remember to plan a menu that will please your eyes and your taste buds. Then you are sure not to go wrong.

4. Planning by the seasons. Chinese food is best when everything is fresh. Try to plan dishes with what's available and good. Asparagus, for example, is one of my favorites, but it's only around for six weeks or so each year. So you have to catch it when it's here—otherwise you'll miss one of the great ones. The growing seasons for vegetables are different for different parts of the country. The thing to do is keep an eye out for good, fresh vegetables because they are the only ones that'll do for good Chinese cooking.

5. The balance of meat and vegetables. The Chinese have always believed in harmony. And I think you know by now what I mean by balance. Not too much of any one thing, but a little bit of a lot of things. Blend the tastes of meats and vegetables so that they are pleasing to your senses as well as your sensibilities. And that's the best way to plan your Chinese menu.

6. Rice and soups are an integral part of any Chinese meal. If you plan to serve a hot (spicy) dish, you might make a bowl of Just Plain Soup (page 127) to help clear the palate. This soup doesn't taste like much, but you won't taste much after eating a hot pepper anyway, so it's useful.

PORK

Some people worship pigs, certain societies have banished them, and some of my closest friends fear them although they have never met one face to face.

The Chinese neither worship pigs nor banish them from their tables. Pigs are very practical household items to every rural family. They occupy very little space, unlike beef cattle, for which much grazing land is required; they'll eat practically any kind of grain, vegetation, roots and leftovers; they are easy to raise—your kids can take care of them; a good sow will produce a litter of ten piglets, and in less than two years the piglets will be big enough to produce their own litters; and every part of the pig is useful—nothing is wasted. Pigs are very efficient, kindly animals, seldom given to fits or malaise if treated properly, and they are extremely good-tasting when cooked properly. It's no wonder that the ancient Chinese domesticated them five thousand years ago!

Pork and chicken are the favorite meats of the Chinese people, and the reasons are quite practical. Both animals can be raised in small spaces. Chicken coops that are four feet wide, eight feet long and four feet high can house up to twenty chickens. Similar space can house one sow and her litter. In a country where most of the land is used for cultivation of rice, vegetables and other crops, these two animals are best suited to the Chinese way of life. On a two- or three-acre farm, you can plant the entire acreage with rice and vegetables and save your back yard for pigs and chickens.

Another reason pork is a favorite among Chinese is that the meat will take on the flavor of the most subtle sauce. Chicken meat behaves in the same way; lamb and beef do not. The flavor of lamb is extremely strong, and for that reason there are relatively few ways to prepare it. You have to create sauces that complement the meat; they must never conflict with each other.

For example, we never cook pork with curry. The reason is this: the meat fibers in pork are very fine (versus beef and chicken fibers which are rather coarse) so the meat will absorb too much of the curry. It will take on too much of the taste, and the result will be disastrous. Not only will you have lost the delicate pork flavor, but you will have lost the consistency of the meat. It's almost like eating raw curry. But curried beef or chicken—now that's something else. Curry works with coarse-fibered meat, because the strong curry flavor will not penetrate all the way through the meat, even when the meat is cut rather thin. (When you cook curried chicken, break open a piece of white meat and you'll see what I mean. Although the curry

will penetrate somewhat, the inside will still be white. That's assuming you've cut the meat into cubes and not into very thin slices.)

When you cook pork the Chinese way, you'll either be cutting the meat into thin slices, or dicing it very fine (ground pork is easier), or just leaving the pork whole, as in pork shoulders or knuckles.

The major cooking characteristic you have to keep in mind is the fine, fibrous nature of the meat. The ideal sauce is the sauce that complements the meat, not one that buries it. For example, when you roast pork (page 18) the idea is to bring out the natural flavor of pork. The taste and smell of roast pork are unique. You should never serve hot mustard with roast pork because the mustard will overwhelm the pork taste. Should you wish to serve mustard, then there is no reason to make the pork dish—you may as well have a hot dog with lots of mustard. (I have seen people order perfectly good roast pork and then bathe it in mustard. That kind of thing just makes me cringe. I wonder why they bother ordering it in the first place! For those of you who are addicted to Chinese mustard—and I have a friend who loves the stuff and puts it on everything Chinese—you should order or cook dishes that go naturally with it.)

Be kind to pork. You don't have to worry about cooking it to death out of fear, and you don't have to overdo any sauce that goes with it. The pork will cook quickly all the way through because you have sliced it very thin or diced it very fine.

Fast cooking is desirable because of the nature of the pork fibers. If you overcook pork, it will be dry and stringy, even if it's cooked in a beautiful sauce. The sauce will hide the stringiness somewhat, but you'll know the difference between right and wrong once you've done it a few times.

Pork and chicken are similar in that, when overcooked, they will get stringy and fall apart. Beef won't fall apart because the lean meat is laced with fat fibers and held together by them. But it too will get stringy when overcooked. It's more difficult to cook pork or chicken because the meat is not laced with fatty tissue. You have to cook it almost exactly right: undercooked, it will be slightly pink, and overcooked it will be dry and stringy. To cook well takes practice, a good, intuitive sense of timing, and the courage to know when to stop—the courage to take the meat out a few seconds sooner than later.

Pigs are tender creatures not to be worshiped, banished, or feared—just cooked properly and enjoyed enormously.

SWEET-AND-SOUR SPARE RIBS

ingredients

3 pounds spare ribs
½ cup water
4 tablespoons sugar
5 tablespoons vinegar
2 tablespoons cornstarch or flour
2 cups water
½ cup soy sauce
1 teaspoon salt
1 teaspoon sugar
3 tablespoons dry sherry

Total prep & cooking time: 1½ hours

to prepare

1
Ask the butcher to cut the ribs into 1-inch pieces—or do it yourself with a cleaver and wooden mallet.

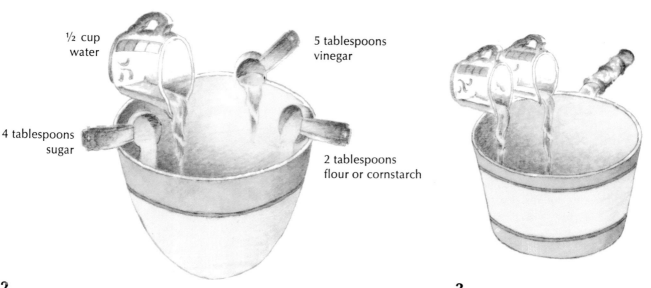

½ cup water

5 tablespoons vinegar

4 tablespoons sugar

2 tablespoons flour or cornstarch

2
Mix well.

3
Put 2 cups water in a deep saucepan.

to cook

1
Bring the water to a boil over a high flame. Add the ribs, ½ cup soy sauce, and 1 teaspoon salt.

2
Bring to a boil again and allow to boil for a minute, then reduce flame to low and simmer for 1 hour. Do not cover the saucepan. Stir now and then.

3
Pour the ribs with the liquid from the saucepan into a large frying pan.

4
Put the frying pan over a high flame. Add 1 teaspoon sugar and 3 tablespoons dry sherry. Stir.

5
Cook over a high flame until almost all of the liquid has evaporated. Stir the ribs now and then to speed evaporation.

6
Now pour in the sauce you've already prepared. Pour slowly, stirring at the same time.

7
Stir-cook for 2 to 3 minutes until the sauce is thick and smooth.

8
Turn off the fire and stir for 30 seconds. Serve.

ROAST PORK

ingredients

1 pound lean pork loin
2 scallions
2 cloves garlic
4 tablespoons soy sauce
4 tablespoons dry sherry
2 tablespoons honey
2 tablespoons catsup
¼ teaspoon ground ginger
water
1 package of large paper clips

This dish is one of my favorites, and I don't always take 2 hours to marinate the meat. When I'm in a hurry, I marinate the meat for 10 minutes on each side.

Total prep & cooking time: 3½ hours

to prepare

1
Cut the pork into 4-inch-long strips, about 1 inch wide and 1 inch high.

2
Crush 2 cloves of garlic and dice with a knife.

3
Cut the scallions into 1-inch pieces.

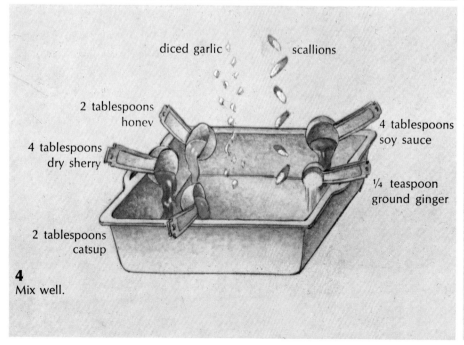

diced garlic   scallions

2 tablespoons honey

4 tablespoons dry sherry

4 tablespoons soy sauce

¼ teaspoon ground ginger

2 tablespoons catsup

4
Mix well.

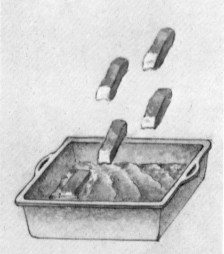

5
Lay pork strips in the sauce. Marinate on one side for 1 hour. Turn over and marinate for 1 more hour.

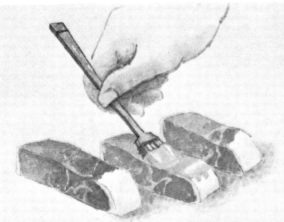

6
Take the pork out and brush the meat lightly and evenly with additional honey.

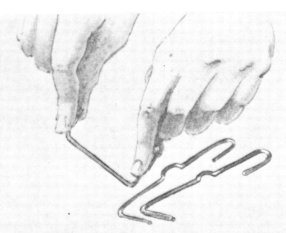

7
Take some large paper clips and bend them out.

8
Hook 1 strip of pork to each paper-clip hook.

9
Put 3 cups water in a large flat pan. Put the pan in the oven. The pan will catch the pork drippings and the steaming water will keep the meat moist.

to cook

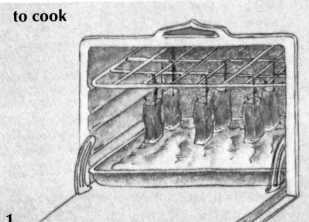

1
Hang the pork strips on an oven rack above the pan. Roast for 35 to 40 minutes at 350°—40 minutes if you have cut the pork thicker than 1 inch.

2
Make sure there's plenty of water in the pan. Add a cup or two more if the level gets low. Brush some marinade on the pork every 10 minutes. Roast for another 15 minutes at 450°; roast only 10 minutes if pork is less than 1 inch thick. Don't let the meat get black around the edges—dark brown is OK. Take the meat out, remove the hooks, and serve.

SPARE RIBS

ingredients

3 pounds spare ribs
6 tablespoons honey
4 tablespoons catsup
3 tablespoons soy sauce

Total prep & cooking time: 40 minutes

Using this recipe, you can barbecue the ribs outdoors on your charcoal broiler. The cooking time should be about the same—depending on the hotness of the charcoal fire. These are finger licking good.

to prepare

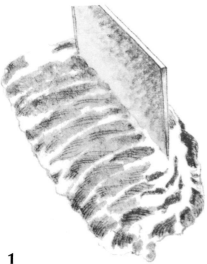

1
Cut off the thick, meaty ends of the ribs (do it yourself or get your butcher to do it).

2
Mix 6 tablespoons honey with 4 tablespoons catsup and 3 tablespoons soy sauce in a large bowl. Mix well.

3
Put the slabs of ribs in the sauce. Smear the sauce liberally over the ribs—it's more fun if you use your fingers.

to cook

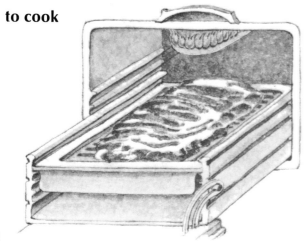

1
Set your broiler on medium-high flame. Place your broiling pan about 4 inches below the flame. Cook the ribs for 7 minutes on each side. Then cook them again for 5 minutes on each side. Cooking time will vary depending on the thickness of the meat.

2
Cut between the ribs and serve. If you are cooking the thick, meaty sections of the ribs too, leave them under the fire longer. Just don't let the meat turn black. Little black strips along the edges are OK, but no more.

PORK WITH GREEN PEAS

ingredients

2 loin end pork chops (½ to ¾ pound)
1 tablespoon oil
1 cup fresh green peas (about 1 pound with shells)
¾ cup water
½ teaspoon salt
¼ teaspoon pepper
¼ cup water
1 tablespoon flour

to prepare

Total prep & cooking time: 20 minutes

Cut meat into thin strips.

to cook

1
Pour 1 tablespoon oil into a frying pan. Set over medium heat. When the oil is hot, add sliced pork. Stir-cook for 2 minutes.

2
Add the peas and stir for 2 minutes.

3
Add ¾ cup water, ½ teaspoon salt, ¼ teaspoon pepper. Stir well for 5 seconds.

4
Reduce flame to low, cover pan, and simmer for 5 minutes.

5
Add the mixture of ¼ cup water and 1 tablespoon flour, stirring as you do so.

6
Stir until the gravy is thick and smooth. Serve.

STEAMED GROUND PORK WITH WATER CHESTNUTS AND EGG

ingredients

1 egg
½ pound ground pork tenderloin
2 tablespoons soy sauce
1 small can water chestnuts
¼ teaspoon salt

Total prep & cooking time: 35 minutes

to prepare

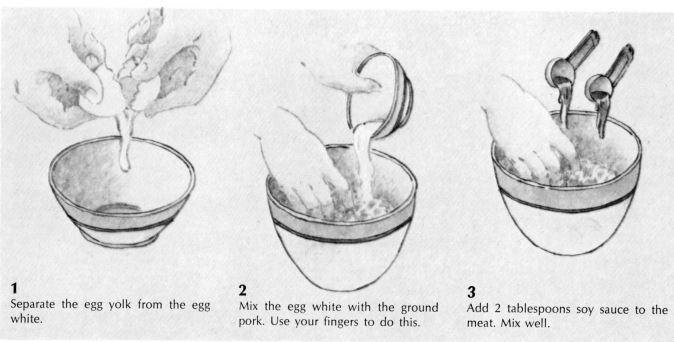

1
Separate the egg yolk from the egg white.

2
Mix the egg white with the ground pork. Use your fingers to do this.

3
Add 2 tablespoons soy sauce to the meat. Mix well.

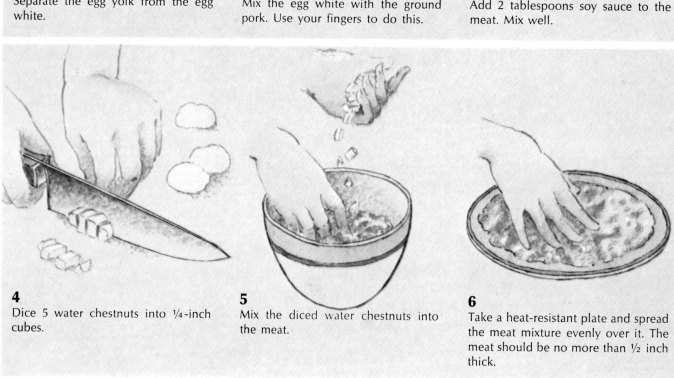

4
Dice 5 water chestnuts into ¼-inch cubes.

5
Mix the diced water chestnuts into the meat.

6
Take a heat-resistant plate and spread the meat mixture evenly over it. The meat should be no more than ½ inch thick.

7
Sprinkle ¼ teaspoon salt evenly over the meat.

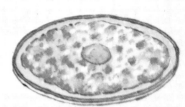

8
Place the egg yolk in the center of the meat. Try not to break the yolk. If it breaks, it's OK, just leave it as it lays.

to cook

Take 3 pieces of wood, each 2 inches high, and place them in the water— or use a metal rack if you have one.

1
Into a large saucepan (big enough for the plate to fit into with an inch all around to spare) pour water to a depth of 1 inch.

2

3
Set the plate on the wood or metal rack. Make sure that the plate is not touching the water in the saucepan.

4
Turn flame to high and bring the water to a boil.

5
Once it starts to boil, turn the flame to medium-low and cover the saucepan. Steam for 20 minutes.

6
Wear gloves when taking out the plate. Serve from the plate.

HOT SPICED PORK

ingredients

4 loin end pork chops
6 hot green peppers (fresh)
¼ cup water
1 teaspoon cornstarch or flour
2 tablespoons oil
2 tablespoons soy sauce
¼ teaspoon salt

Total prep & cooking time: 20 minutes

Six hot green peppers are *really* hot; three are enough for those of you who like it hot; and one is enough for those who are not at all used to hot food.

to prepare

1
Cut the pork into thin slices, from 1 to 2 inches long—but all should have the same thickness.

2
Cut the hot green peppers into ¼ inch rings.

3
Mix ¼ cup water with 1 teaspoon cornstarch or flour.

4
Put 2 tablespoons oil into a frying pan.

to cook

1
Use a high flame to heat the oil.

2
When the oil is hot, add the sliced pork. Reduce flame to medium. Stir for 2 minutes.

3
Add the hot green peppers. Stir for 1 minute.

4
Add 2 tablespoons soy sauce and ¼ teaspoon salt. Stir for 1 minute.

5
Slowly add some of the water/cornstarch mixture. Stir. Continue to add and stir until the sauce is thick and smooth—takes about a minute.

6
Turn off flame. Stir the pork with hot peppers a few times. Serve.

RED-COOKED PORK

ingredients

5- to 7-pound fresh pork shoulder
1 pound fresh spinach
4 cups water
2 cups soy sauce
¼ teaspoon ground ginger
3 tablespoons sugar
⅓ cup dry sherry

Total prep & cooking time: 4½ hours

This dish is great when you want to feed a large group of people. You can start it in the afternoon and it'll be cooked by dinnertime. This plus three other dishes (say one from each section) will feed 6 hungry adults.

to prepare

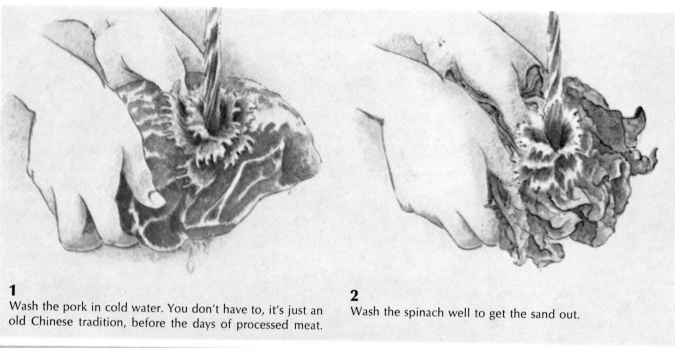

1
Wash the pork in cold water. You don't have to, it's just an old Chinese tradition, before the days of processed meat.

2
Wash the spinach well to get the sand out.

to cook

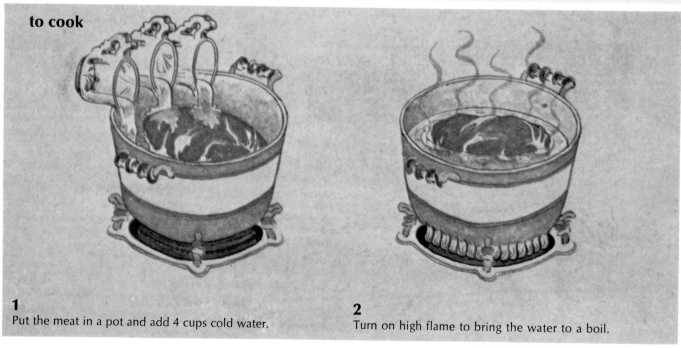

1
Put the meat in a pot and add 4 cups cold water.

2
Turn on high flame to bring the water to a boil.

26

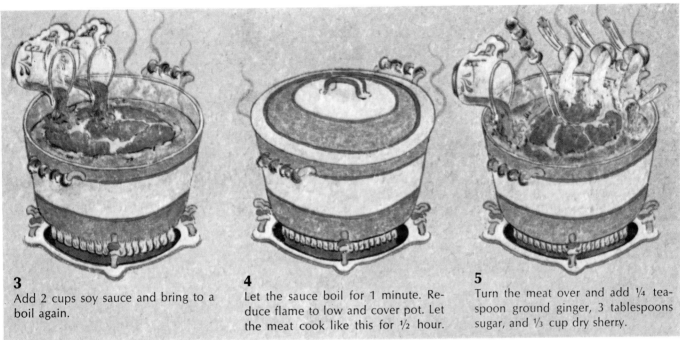

3
Add 2 cups soy sauce and bring to a boil again.

4
Let the sauce boil for 1 minute. Reduce flame to low and cover pot. Let the meat cook like this for ½ hour.

5
Turn the meat over and add ¼ teaspoon ground ginger, 3 tablespoons sugar, and ⅓ cup dry sherry.

6
Turn the meat every ½ hour.

7
Cook the meat over a low flame for about 3 to 4 hours, or ½ hour per pound of meat. You can cook it longer; the meat gets more tender with time.

8
After the meat is cooked, take it out and slice it for serving. Pour some gravy over the sliced meat. Save some gravy for cooking the spinach.

9
Put the spinach into the remaining gravy. Cook over medium heat for 5 minutes. Serve.

PORK WITH BEAN SPROUTS

ingredients

2 loin end pork chops
  (½ to ¾ pound)
¼ cup soy sauce
1 tablespoon sugar
a pinch of ground ginger
2 cups bean sprouts (fresh or
  canned)
2 tablespoons oil
1 teaspoon flour

Total prep & cooking time: 25 minutes

to prepare

1
Slice the pork chops into very thin strips, as thin as you can. Throw away the bones unless you want to save them to make soup.

2
Mix ¼ cup soy sauce, 1 tablespoon sugar, and a pinch of ground ginger in a bowl. Mix well.

3
Add the sliced pork to the sauce. Stir the pork in the sauce until thoroughly coated. Let it sit for a few minutes.

4
Wash the bean sprouts under cold water. Leave in the colander to drain.

to cook

1
Put a frying pan over medium-high flame. Add 2 tablespoons oil to pan. Let the oil get hot. (Oil is hot enough when a drop of water sizzles in it.)

2
Pour the pork and sauce into the pan.

3
Stir-cook the pork for 3 to 4 minutes. Keep stirring the pork, keeping it in motion so the heat gets at it evenly.

4
Stir in 1 teaspoon flour. Stir it well for 4 to 5 seconds.

5
Add 2 cups bean sprouts.

6
Stir-cook the bean sprouts and pork for 3 minutes. Serve.

SWEET-AND-SOUR PORK

ingredients

1 pound boneless pork shoulder
½ cup flour
1 egg
½ teaspoon salt
4 tablespoons water
1 cup pineapple cubes
1 green pepper
1 carrot
¾ cup vinegar

¼ cup brown sugar
1½ tablespoons molasses
2 tablespoons cornstarch
peanut oil for deep frying

Total prep & cooking time: 45 minutes

to prepare

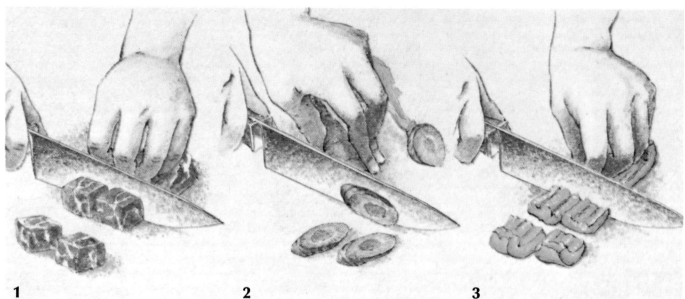

1
Cut the pork into 1-inch cubes.

2
Cut the carrot into ⅛-inch slices, using the crosscut.

3
Cut the green pepper into 1-inch squares, discarding the seeds.

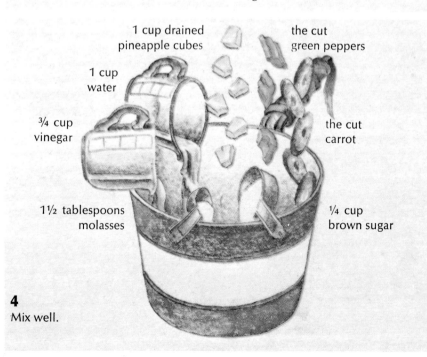

1 cup drained pineapple cubes

1 cup water

¾ cup vinegar

1½ tablespoons molasses

the cut green peppers

the cut carrot

¼ cup brown sugar

4
Mix well.

5
Take ¼ cup water, add 2 tablespoons cornstarch, and mix.

6
In a mixing bowl, combine ½ cup flour, 1 egg, ½ teaspoon salt, and 4 tablespoons water. Mix into a batter.

7
Dip pork cubes into the batter. Each cube should be completely covered. Remove cubes from batter and put on a plate.

to cook

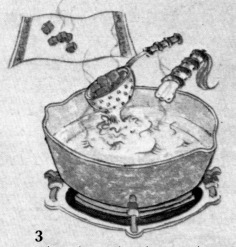

1
In a deep frying pan pour oil to a depth of about 1½ inches. Turn on high flame.

2
When the oil is very hot (when a drop of water sizzles in it) add the batter-covered pork cubes.

3
When the pork cubes are brown, take them out and drain on paper towels. Use a slotted spoon—or chopsticks. Browning takes about 4 minutes.

4
Put the saucepan containing the vinegar, sugar, molasses, pineapple, and vegetables over a medium flame. Stir mixture until it bubbles.

5
When the sauce bubbles (boils), add the ¼ cup water/cornstarch mixture. Stir until the sauce is thick and smooth.

6
Add the deep-fried pork cubes to this lovely sauce. Reduce flame to low. Cover pan and simmer for 10 minutes. Serve.

SLICED PORK WITH GREEN PEPPERS

ingredients

1 pound loin end pork chops
3 green peppers
2 tablespoons soy sauce
1 tablespoon dry sherry
1 teaspoon honey
1 teaspoon salt
1 tablespoon cornstarch
2 tablespoons water
3 tablespoons oil
salt and pepper to taste   Total prep & cooking time: 30 minutes

to prepare

1
Slice the pork into thin strips about 1½ inches long.

2
Cut the green peppers into 1-inch squares. Throw away the seeds.

3
Make a marinade with 2 tablespoons soy sauce, 1 table-spoon dry sherry, 1 teaspoon honey, 1 teaspoon salt, 1 tablespoon cornstarch, 2 tablespoons water. Mix well.

4
Put the sliced pork in the marinade. Mix well.   Let stand for 10 minutes.

to cook

1
Put 2 tablespoons oil in a frying pan over a high flame.

2
When the oil is hot, add the cut green peppers. Stir-cook for 2 minutes.

3
Take the pan off the fire and put the green peppers on a plate. You'll cook them again in a few minutes.

4
Add 1 tablespoon oil to the frying pan and heat.

5
Take the meat out of the sauce and put the meat in the hot pan. Stir for 1 minute.

6
Add the green peppers that you've put on the plate. Stir for 1 minute.

7
Add the marinade sauce to the pan. Stir until the sauce is thick and hot.

8
Add salt and pepper for taste. Stir a few times. Serve.

PORK WITH HOT PEPPERS, SZECHUAN STYLE

ingredients

- 4 loin end pork chops
- 4 scallions
- 2 dry red peppers (the hot kind)
- 2 cloves garlic
- 4 tablespoons catsup
- ¼ teaspoon ground ginger
- 2 tablespoons dry sherry
- 1 teaspoon sugar
- ¼ cup water
- 1 teaspoon cornstarch or flour
- 2 tablespoons peanut oil

Total prep & cooking time: 20 minutes

to prepare

1
Cut the pork chops into thin strips.

2
Cut the scallions into 1-inch pieces.

3
Crush the 2 cloves of garlic and dice with a knife.

4
Cut the 2 hot peppers into ½-inch pieces.

5
Mix 4 tablespoons catsup, ¼ teaspoon ground ginger, 2 tablespoons dry sherry, and 1 teaspoon sugar.

6
Mix ¼ cup water with 1 teaspoon cornstarch or flour.

to cook

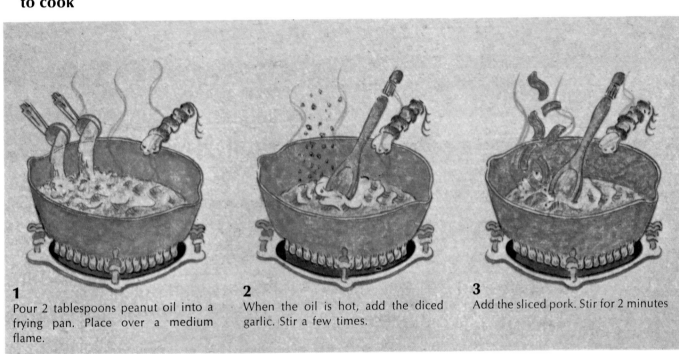

1
Pour 2 tablespoons peanut oil into a frying pan. Place over a medium flame.

2
When the oil is hot, add the diced garlic. Stir a few times.

3
Add the sliced pork. Stir for 2 minutes

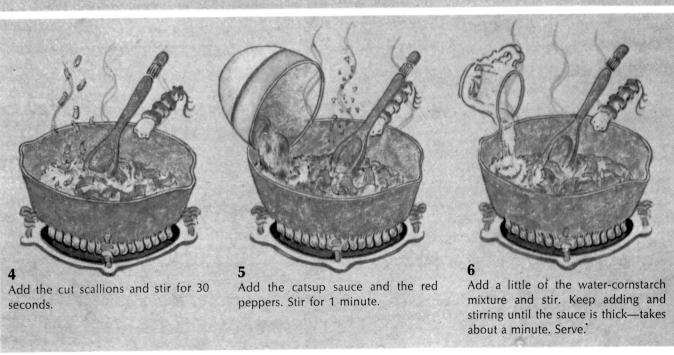

4
Add the cut scallions and stir for 30 seconds.

5
Add the catsup sauce and the red peppers. Stir for 1 minute.

6
Add a little of the water-cornstarch mixture and stir. Keep adding and stirring until the sauce is thick—takes about a minute. Serve.

GROUND PORK WITH STRING BEANS

ingredients

- 1 pound green beans
- 1 clove garlic
- 1 tablespoon cornstarch or flour
- 2¼ cups water
- 1 tablespoon oil
- 1 pound lean ground pork
- 2 tablespoons soy sauce
- ¼ teaspoon salt

Total prep & cooking time: 25 minutes

This dish is enough for two adults and one child. Try serving it over rice. Cut this recipe in half if you plan to have other dishes. Don't overcook the beans. Bite into a piece after 3-4 minutes of cooking to check crispness. The thicker the beans, the longer it takes to cook. But whatever you do, don't cook the crispness out.

to prepare

1
Wash the green beans and break off the ends.

2
Crush the garlic and chop fine with a knife.

3
Add a tablespoon of cornstarch or flour to ¼ cup water.

4
Bring 2 cups of water to a boil and have it ready.

to cook

1
Add 1 tablespoon oil to a frying pan. Use medium heat.

2
Add the diced garlic to the hot oil. Stir a few times.

3
Add the ground pork and stir-cook for 5 minutes.

4
Add 2 tablespoons soy sauce and ¼ teaspoon salt, stirring all the while. Stir for 2 minutes.

5
Add the uncut green beans. Mix well for 1 minute.

6
Now slowly pour in about a cup of the boiling water that you have ready. Mix well.

7
When the sauce boils again, turn the flame to low and simmer for 6 to 8 minutes depending on thickness of the beans. Stir now and then.

8
Slowly add the ¼ cup water/cornstarch mixture. Stir and add until the sauce thickens—takes about a minute. (You don't have to use all the water/cornstarch mixture.) Serve.

SHANGHAI STYLE PORK CHOPS

ingredients

½ cup flour
1 egg
½ teaspoon salt
4 tablespoons water
4 center cut pork chops
   (about ½-inch-thick chops)
4 tablespoons soy sauce
2 tablespoons honey

3 tablespoons catsup
4 tablespoons water
2 tablespoons flour
peanut oil

Total prep & cooking time: 30 minutes

to prepare

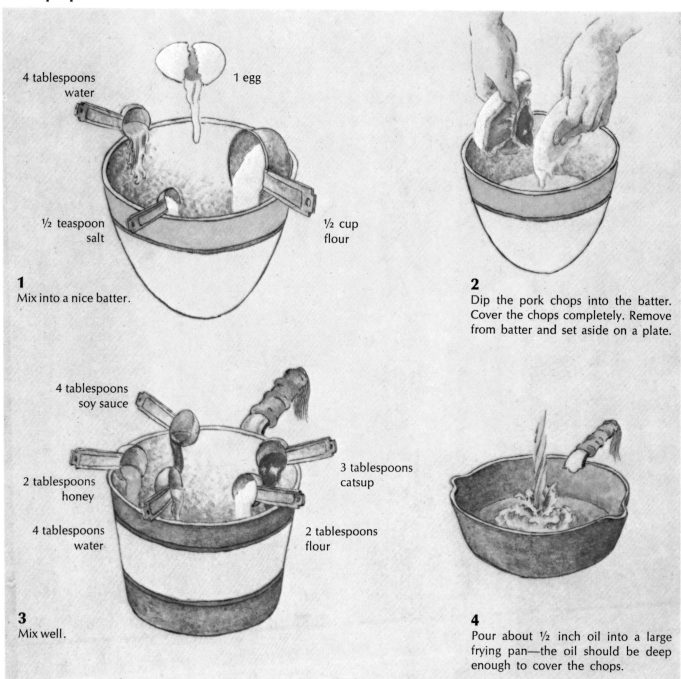

4 tablespoons water

1 egg

½ teaspoon salt

½ cup flour

1
Mix into a nice batter.

2
Dip the pork chops into the batter. Cover the chops completely. Remove from batter and set aside on a plate.

4 tablespoons soy sauce

2 tablespoons honey

4 tablespoons water

3 tablespoons catsup

2 tablespoons flour

3
Mix well.

4
Pour about ½ inch oil into a large frying pan—the oil should be deep enough to cover the chops.

to cook

1
Heat the oil in the frying pan over a high flame. The oil is hot enough when a drop of water sizzles in it. Put the pork chops in the hot oil.

2
Reduce flame to medium and cook until the chops are brown—about 4 minutes. Turn the chops over once during this time.

3
Take the chops out and drain on paper towels.

4
Over a low flame, heat the sauce in the large saucepan, stirring it until it is thick and creamy—about 2 minutes.

5
Now add the chops.

6
Let the chops simmer in the sauce for 5 minutes. Make sure the chops are immersed in the sauce. Serve.

STEWED PORK WITH TURNIPS

ingredients

- 2 pounds pork loin
- 1 pound white turnips (3 or 4 medium-sized turnips)
- 1½ cups water
- ¾ cup soy sauce
- 3 tablespoons dry sherry
- ¼ teaspoon ground ginger
- 1 tablespoon sugar

Total prep & cooking time: 2½ hours

to prepare

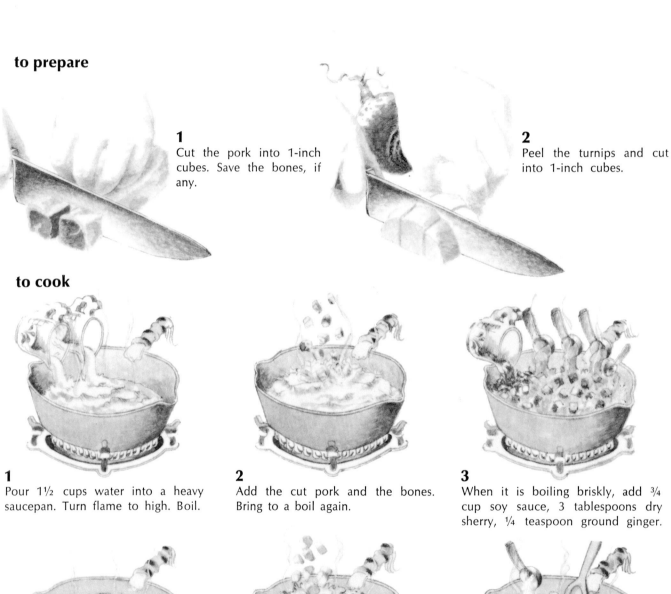

1
Cut the pork into 1-inch cubes. Save the bones, if any.

2
Peel the turnips and cut into 1-inch cubes.

to cook

1
Pour 1½ cups water into a heavy saucepan. Turn flame to high. Boil.

2
Add the cut pork and the bones. Bring to a boil again.

3
When it is boiling briskly, add ¾ cup soy sauce, 3 tablespoons dry sherry, ¼ teaspoon ground ginger.

4
Bring to a boil again. Reduce flame to low. Cover pan and simmer for 1 hour.

5
Add the cut turnips. Cover pan and simmer for ½ hour.

6
Add 1 tablespoon sugar and stir the sauce. Cover pan and simmer for ½ hour more. Serve in deep bowl.

This book is written for the single person who is tired of eating out; for the person who likes to cook Chinese food but can't always get the authentic ingredients; for the person who has never cooked Chinese food before; for the person who has never cooked before; and for the housewife who needs to feed a family elegantly and inexpensively.

soy sauces

Whatever category you belong to, let me warn you about the use of soy sauces. It has been my experience that imported soy sauces are much milder in flavor than the domestic brands. Some domestic brands are almost *four* times as strong as the imports. This has its advantages because you can use less of a domestic soy sauce and save money. What I would suggest is that you buy the brand that's usually available at your supermarket, then experiment with it. That is, cook one dish and adjust the amount as necessary. If the dish turns out too salty, try cutting the soy sauce by diluting it with water. Experiment until it tastes good, then remember to adjust your recipes according to the strength of the brand you buy. I used the imported brands in the preparation of this book.

cooking utensils

Here's what you'd need in way of cooking utensils:
   one 10-inch frying pan (preferably cast-iron)
   one medium-sized saucepan with lid for cooking rice
   one 9-inch-diameter (or larger) pot for cooking stews, pork shoulder, fish
   a small spatula for stir-frying (big ones are harder to handle)
   a sharp knife or cleaver
   some bowls of various sizes or a set of mixing bowls

That should be enough for you to get started. You won't need any more unless you decide to cook a large meal for more than three people. For you recently divorced people, this is one way to furnish a kitchen inexpensively.

no exotic utensils needed

The Chinese Wok was designed to fit into a large circular hole in the Chinese stove. It sits almost flush with the top of the stove so that the fire heats the entire bottom of the Wok. The American stove was not designed for that, and in fact, the traditional cast iron frying pan works better than the Wok because it gets the full benefit of the flames. The heat tends to localize in the area immediately above the flame, and the thin metal of the Wok doesn't distribute the heat as well. But the thick, cast iron frying pan will distribute the heat much better. Personally, I prefer the cast iron frying pan when I cook on the American stove.

what to cook first?

It's always hard to decide what to cook first when you get a new cookbook. It's even harder if you've never cooked Chinese food before. Here are some suggestions to get you started on the right foot:
Ground Pork with String Beans
Spare Ribs
Roast Pork
White-Cooked Chicken in Wine
White-Cooked Chicken Dipped in Hot Sauce
Chicken with Asparagus
Crabmeat with Eggs
Shrimps with Peas
Shrimps in Hot Sauce
Beef with Broccoli
Beef with Asparagus
Barbecued Beef
Cucumber Soup
Watercress and Chicken Giblet Soup

ask your butcher

If you want to make spare ribs or lobsters but can't motivate yourself to chop them up (especially those live lobsters), ask your friendly butcher to chop them up for you. You'll have to tell him how you want them cut. Most butchers are not accustomed to cutting ribs or lobsters into small, bite-sized pieces. But if you show them how, they are usually happy to do it.

what to buy

Buy the cheapest cuts of meat possible, especially pork. You generally don't have to worry about the tenderness of the meat because you'll slice it very thin anyway. And no matter how tough the meat is, when sliced and cooked the Chinese way, it'll be tender—and money-saving, too. Start out using my suggestions, then try different cuts and see if you notice the difference between an inexpensive cut and an expensive one.

preparation

If you want to cook, say, three stir-fry dishes, then prepare everything in advance. Complete all the preparation steps; then you'll be able to zip through the dishes in no time.

POULTRY

As you can see, I've organized this book with pork and poultry in first and second place, respectively. It's a toss-up as to which is more popular, but I think most people would agree that pork is the most popular meat in China. In any case, one thing is certain: beef is the last meat on the list, not because it's unpopular, but because there's not much beef cattle around.

But chicken! Chinese cooks have created innumerable ways of cooking chicken. A particularly unique way is White-Cooked Chicken. This is where you put the chicken in boiling water for 15 minutes, then turn *off* the fire and let the chicken cook in the hot water for 20 more minutes. This very basic way of cooking chicken keeps the chicken fresh, tender, and juicy. Because you don't keep it in the boiling water long, the chicken retains its natural juices. You are not cooking the juice out of it, so to speak—and the broth is watery. (To get a nice, rich chicken broth, you'd have to cook all of the chicken juice out of the chicken and into the broth. That's why the chicken meat in the chicken soup is dry and stringy . . . all the good, natural juices went into the water to make the broth.) The idea is to avoid overcooking (which is the basic concept for all Chinese food). Of course, the cooking time will vary depending on the weight of the chicken. Most supermarket chickens that weigh 2 to 3 pounds are young and tender. You can't really go wrong with any brand that's available.

The thing to look at in choosing a chicken is the drumsticks: a chicken with thin drumsticks will cook faster than one with fat drumsticks, but the latter will be juicier.

For those of you who are beginners and have never encountered a chicken, or learned how to cut it up, take heart. In the Curried Chicken recipe, there are complete illustrations for cutting up a whole chicken. Use those illustrations wherever you run across a recipe that directs you to cut up a whole chicken—or a duck, for that matter. They're about the same.

There are a number of interesting things that I've learned about cooking while writing this book. And here's a good place to pass them along to you.

When I first started to cook in a serious way (that is, to feed myself three or four good meals a week), I had a difficult time keeping up with the cookbooks. Trying to find step 7 in a paragraph of type while stir-frying is not conducive to a good performance. That's where I hope this book will help you. You will be able to find step 7 at a glance, and the picture is worth a thousand words. You can stir-fry and keep up with the book without panicking. (The best way to use this book is to study the recipe and pictures. Then imagine in your own mind how to do the dish. Put the book aside and try to cook the dish from memory. Glance at the book now and then just to confirm your steps, and to get some confidence.)

After a few tries at a particular dish, forget about the book and simply make your own list of ingredients. Then try to make the dish from these. And when the dish becomes reasonably successful, you can make it from memory. After a while, you won't need a cookbook at all unless it's to try something you've never made before.

When I started to write this book, I discovered that I didn't have the vaguest idea of the amount of ingredients for each dish—or precisely how long I had to cook each dish. I had gotten so accustomed to cooking by eye that I found it hard to cook any other way. For example, if I saw a fresh, good-looking sea bass at the fish market, I'd buy it. I didn't follow a cookbook and hunt down a 1-pounder; I got a sea bass. (When I first started cooking, I worried a lot about the weight of the meat or fish. I was much too anxious to have everything just right to realize that I could simply adjust the proportions of the rest of the ingredients to the main one.)

Later on, I grew more relaxed about this. When I got the sea bass (or whatever) home, I'd line up all the ingredients needed, or if I didn't have everything, I'd forget about it and make the fish anyway—as long as I wasn't lacking a major ingredient.

Cooking by eye simply means "a little of this and a little of that." And when it looked cooked, it usually was cooked. For this book, I had to go back and measure out each ingredient. And trying to measure exact proportions wasn't the easiest task. (It was a lot easier to do a little of this and a little of that.)

I had a comparable problem with timing. Trying to cook and use a stopwatch at the same time is not much fun. The scene would go something like this: I'd start the stopwatch, throw in the sliced chicken and start stir-frying. When the chicken looked cooked, I'd take my spatula and cut a piece of chicken in half to check the inside. Once confirmed, I'd put everything down and click off the stopwatch, then hurry back to the chicken and scoop it out of the pan.

From this experience, I can visualize your problem, but in reverse. My advice is this: Don't watch the clock or the sweeping second hand; use your eye to determine when something is done, and cut into a piece of meat now and again to confirm the cooking time. After a while you'll develop an intuitive feel for cooking Chinese food. Another way to do it is to follow the steps and count off the seconds to yourself. Do this often enough and you'll soon be able to tell exactly when any dish is cooked.

WHITE-COOKED CHICKEN IN WINE

ingredients

1 whole chicken (2 to 3 pounds)
1 cup of your favorite white wine

Use 1 tablespoon of salt mixed with ¾ tablespoon of ground black pepper as a dip for the chicken.

Make this dish the night before a picnic. Marinate overnight in the refrigerator.

Total prep & cooking time: 2 hours

to prepare

Wash the chicken, take off the fat.

to cook

1
Put 4 quarts of water in a large saucepan. Bring the water to a boil over a high flame.

2
Put the chicken in the boiling water and boil for 15 minutes.

3
Turn off the flame and let the chicken sit in the hot water for 20 more minutes.

4
Take the chicken out and put it in the refrigerator for ½ hour.

5
Remove the chicken from the refrigerator and pull the meat off the bones. Cut the meat into 2-inch pieces. Arrange the meat on a deep plate.

6
Pour 1 cup of your favorite white wine over the chicken. Let it marinate for at least ½ hour in the refrigerator—the longer the better. Serve cold, with salt-and-pepper dip on the side.

COLD CHICKEN WITH HOT PEPPER SAUCE

ingredients

1 2- to 3-pound chicken
4 tablespoons soy sauce
½ teaspoon crushed red pepper
3 tablespoons peanut oil

Add more crushed red pepper if you like it hot

Total prep & cooking time: 2½ hours

to prepare

Wash the chicken.

to cook

1
Put 4 quarts water in a deep saucepan. Bring to a boil.
Put the chicken in the boiling water. Bring to a boil again.

2
Reduce the heat to low, cover the pan and simmer for 1¼ hours. Then take chicken out and put it in the refrigerator for ½ hour.

3
Pull the meat off the chicken and cut it into 2-inch pieces. Arrange the meat on a plate and put it back in the refrigerator. Take the chicken out when it's completely cold.

3 tablespoons peanut oil

4 tablespoons soy sauce

½ teaspoon crushed red pepper

4
Mix well.

5
Heat the hot pepper sauce in a small saucepan over a medium fire for 1 minute.

6
Pour the heated hot pepper sauce over the chicken. Serve.

CHICKEN WITH ASPARAGUS

ingredients

1 chicken breast
½ cup chicken broth
1 teaspoon cornstarch
1 tablespoon dry sherry
1 teaspoon salt
¼ teaspoon ground ginger
1 pound fresh asparagus
4 tablespoons vegetable oil

Total prep & cooking time: 20 minutes

to prepare

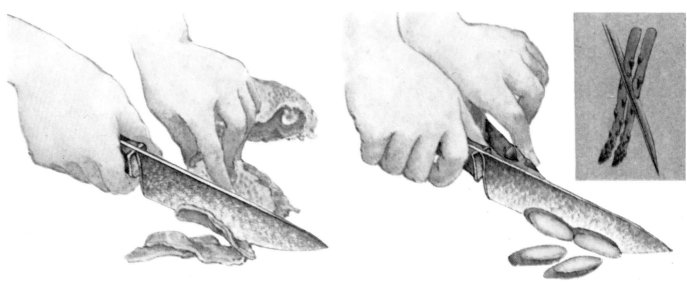

1
Slice the chicken into thin slices about 1 to 2 inches long.

2
Cut the asparagus with the famous Chinese crosscut (wash them first).

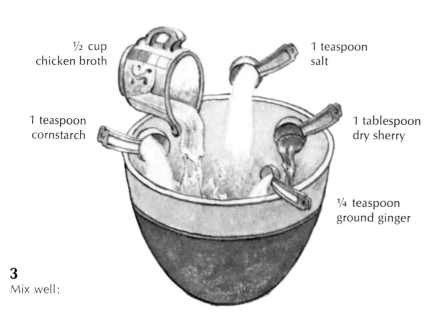

½ cup chicken broth

1 teaspoon salt

1 teaspoon cornstarch

1 tablespoon dry sherry

¼ teaspoon ground ginger

3
Mix well:

4
Mix the sliced chicken with the sauce.

to cook

1
Put 2 tablespoons vegetable oil in a frying pan. Turn flame to high.

2
When the oil is hot, add the cut asparagus. Stir rapidly for 2 minutes. Shake a little salt on it.

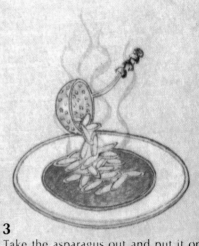

3
Take the asparagus out and put it on a plate. Set aside.

4
Put 2 additional tablespoons oil in the frying pan. Turn flame to high.

5
When the oil is hot, add the sliced chicken and the sauce to the pan. Stir for 2 minutes.

6
Add the asparagus to the chicken. Stir for 1 to 1½ minutes. Serve.

CAULIFLOWER IN CHICKEN SAUCE

ingredients

1½ pounds cauliflower
1 chicken breast (about ½ pound)
3 egg whites
1 teaspoon cornstarch
1 teaspoon salt
2 tablespoons water
2 tablespoons oil
2 strips of bacon (optional)

Total prep & cooking time: 30 minutes

As a final touch for this recipe, grill 2 pieces of bacon until well done while cooking the chicken. Drain the bacon and break it up into small flakes. Sprinkle on top of the chicken. If you happen to have a small piece of smoked ham around, dice it up and use it instead of the bacon.

to prepare

1
Wash cauliflower and remove green stem and any leaves. Cut the cauliflower into small pieces.

2
Cut the chicken into long, thin strips.

3
Then cut the strips again into small pieces.

4
Put the meat in a pile and chop it. Use a lot of wrist action —it should sound like a machine gun.

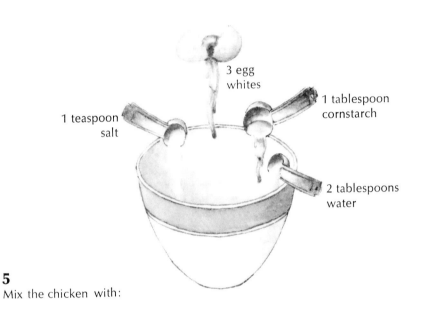

3 egg
whites

1 tablespoon
cornstarch

1 teaspoon
salt

2 tablespoons
water

5
Mix the chicken with:

6
Beat with an egg beater until it's blended.

to cook

1
Put 2 tablespoons oil in a frying pan. Turn on medium-high flame. When the oil is hot, add the chicken. Stir-cook for 2 minutes.

2
Add the cauliflower and stir for 2 minutes. Serve.

CURRIED CHICKEN

ingredients

½ broiling chicken
2 baking potatoes
2 onions
4 tablespoons oil
1½ cups water
4 tablespoons curry powder
1 teaspoon salt

Total prep & cooking time: 1¼ hours

to prepare

1
Cut the thigh from the body of the chicken.

2
Separate the thigh from the drumstick.

3
Cut the wing from the body of the chicken.

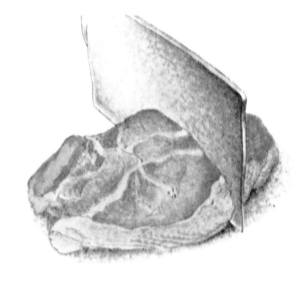

4
Cut the breast into 4 equal parts.

5
Peel the potatoes and cut them into 1-inch cubes.

6
Cut up the onions.

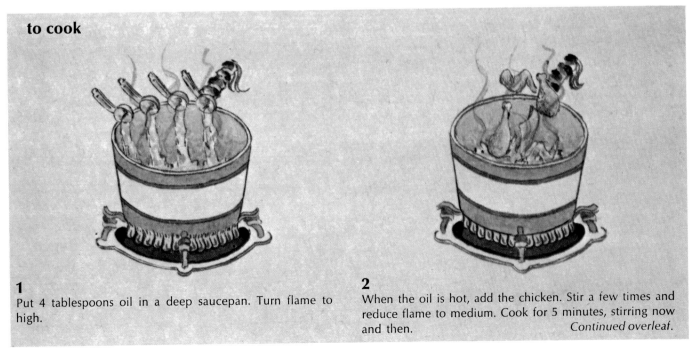

to cook

1
Put 4 tablespoons oil in a deep saucepan. Turn flame to high.

2
When the oil is hot, add the chicken. Stir a few times and reduce flame to medium. Cook for 5 minutes, stirring now and then. *Continued overleaf.*

3
Add 1½ cups water, and turn flame on high. Bring to a boil.

4
Reduce flame to medium, and add 4 tablespoons curry powder. Stir in well for 30 seconds.

5
Add potatoes and 1 teaspoon salt. Stir a few times. Bring to a boil again.

6
After mixture boils, reduce flame to low. Cover the pan and simmer for 20 minutes, stirring now and again.

7
Add the onions. Stir a few times. Cover the pan and simmer for 20 minutes.

8
You can simmer this longer if you like. The sauce gets better as it cooks. Serve in a deep bowl. The curry sauce over rice is terrific!

SOY SAUCE CHICKEN WINGS

ingredients

1 cup soy sauce
2 cups water
3 tablespoons sugar
2½-3 pounds chicken wings
⅓ cup dry sherry

Cooking time: 65 minutes

to cook

1
Put 1 cup soy sauce, 2 cups water, and 3 tablespoons sugar into a large saucepan. Bring sauce to a boil.

2
Put the chicken wings into the boiling sauce.

3
Pour ⅓ cup dry sherry over the chicken and bring to a boil again. Reduce flame to low.

4
Use a low flame and let the sauce bubble gently.

5
Cover pan and cook gently for 1 hour. Turn the wings every 10 minutes or so. You can serve the wings hot or cold. In fact, cold, they're great for midnight snacks!

CHICKEN VELVET

ingredients

1 chicken breast
2 teaspoons cornstarch
½ teaspoon salt
2 egg whites
½ cup water
6 egg whites (that's a total of 8)
½ cup chicken broth
1 tablespoon dry sherry
½ teaspoon salt
1 tablespoon cornstarch
4 tablespoons oil

This is the hardest dish to make (in this book). If you can make this one, you are ready to go on to bigger and better things.

Total prep & cooking time: 45 minutes

to prepare

1
Remove the meat from the chicken breast and chop into small, fine pieces.

2
Using a mortar and pestle, pound chopped chicken into a fine paste. If you don't have a mortar and pestle, put chicken into a bowl and mash with a large spoon. This should take about 10 minutes.

3
Add, a little at a time, 2 teaspoons cornstarch, ½ teaspoon salt, 2 unbeaten egg whites. Each time you add, mash and mix with a spoon.

4
Add ½ cup water, a few drops at a time, mixing well after each addition to make sure water is thoroughly absorbed into the paste.

54

5
Beat 6 egg whites until stiff.

6
Pour the beaten egg whites onto the chicken paste.

7
Fold the chicken paste into the beaten egg whites. Keep folding until egg whites are well incorporated into the paste—so that the two are one.

8
In a small saucepan combine ½ cup chicken broth, 1 tablespoon dry sherry, ½ teaspoon salt, 1 tablespoon cornstarch. Mix well.

to cook

1
Heat the chicken-broth sauce over a medium flame until it becomes thick and clear. Set sauce aside.

2
Add 4 tablespoons oil to large frying pan. Turn flame to high.

3
When the oil is hot, add the chicken paste. Right after the chicken is in the pan, take the pan off the heat!

4
With the pan off the fire, beat the chicken with a fork until the oil is absorbed. Beat as in scrambled eggs.

5
Put the pan back on the high flame for 10 to 15 seconds, or until the mixture starts to set.

6
Put the chicken on a plate and pour off the excess oil. Reheat the sauce and pour it over the chicken. Serve.

CHINESE FRIED CHICKEN

ingredients

1 2-pound chicken
2 tablespoons dry sherry
3 tablespoons soy sauce
3 teaspoons cornstarch
4 quarts water
oil for deep frying

Total prep & cooking time: 1 hour

The quick, deep frying cooks the cornstarch or flour batter that covers the chicken. That's why you can make this dish so quickly.

to prepare

3 tablespoons soy sauce

2 tablespoons dry sherry

3 teaspoons cornstarch

1
Wash the chicken.

2
Mix well.

to cook

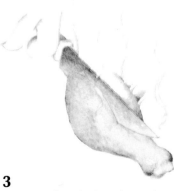

1
Put 4 quarts water in a deep saucepan. Bring it to a boil.

2
Put the chicken in the boiling water. Bring to a boil again. Boil the chicken for 15 minutes. Turn off flame and let chicken sit in the hot water for 15 more minutes.

3
Remove the chicken from the saucepan and cut the meat off the bones in large pieces.

4
Slice the meat into pieces 2 inches long and 1 inch thick. Put the cut chicken on a plate.

5
Stir the sherry/soy sauce/cornstarch mixture again and pour it evenly over the chicken. Each piece should get a thin coat of the mixture.

6
Put about an inch of peanut oil in a frying pan. Turn flame to high.

7
When the oil is hot, put 5 or 6 pieces of chicken in the oil. Deep-fry for 1 minute, or until the chicken is brown and crisp.

8
Take out the cooked pieces and let them drain on paper towels.

9
Put in 5 or 6 more pieces and repeat the process until it's all cooked. Serve.

SHREDDED CHICKEN WITH GREEN PEAS

ingredients

 1 chicken breast
½ cup chicken broth
 2 teaspoons cornstarch
 1 tablespoon dry sherry
1½ teaspoons salt
 2 pounds fresh peas or 1
    package frozen peas
 4 tablespoons peanut oil

Total prep & cooking time: 20 minutes

to prepare

1
Slice the chicken into thin slices about 1 to 2 inches long.

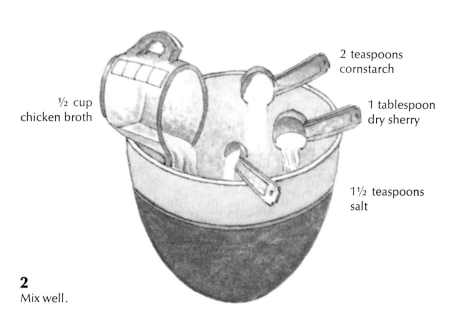

½ cup
chicken broth

2 teaspoons
cornstarch

1 tablespoon
dry sherry

1½ teaspoons
salt

2
Mix well.

3
Mix the sliced chicken with the sauce. If you use frozen peas, let them thaw. Shell the fresh peas.

to cook

1
Put 2 tablespoons oil in a frying pan. Turn flame to high.

2
When the oil is hot, add the peas. Stir rapidly for 1 minute.

3
Take the peas out and put them on a plate. Set aside.

4
Put 2 more tablespoons oil in the frying pan. Turn flame to medium high.

5
When the oil is hot, put the sliced chicken mixed with the sauce in the frying pan. Stir for 3 minutes.

6
Add the peas to the chicken. Stir for 1 minute. Serve.

ROAST CHICKEN

ingredients

1 2-pound chicken
2 cups water
1 cup soy sauce
½ cup dry sherry
1 teaspoon salt
1 tablespoon sugar
½ teaspoon ground ginger

Total prep & cooking time: 70 minutes

to prepare

1 cup
soy sauce

½ cup
dry sherry

2 cups
water

1
Wash the chicken.

2
Pour into a deep saucepan.

to cook

1
Use a high flame to bring the liquid to a boil. Add 1 teaspoon salt, 1 tablespoon sugar, and ½ teaspoon ground ginger.

2
Put the chicken in the boiling liquid.

3
When the liquid boils again, turn the flame low, cover the pan and simmer for 15 minutes.

4
Turn off the fire, turn the chicken over, and let it sit in the broth for 15 minutes.

5
Take the chicken out and let it drain on a plate.

6
Put the chicken in a roasting pan. Preheat the oven to 450°.

7
Put the chicken in the oven to roast for ½ hour. The chicken should be crisp and brown. Serve. Use the sauce as a dip, or serve over rice.

WHITE-COOKED CHICKEN DIPPED IN HOT SAUCE

ingredients

1 2- to 3-pound chicken
2 scallions
2 cloves garlic
4 tablespoons soy sauce
2 tablespoons honey
½ teaspoon salt
3 quarts water
3 tablespoons oil
¼ teaspoon ground ginger
½ teaspoon crushed red peppe

Total prep & cooking time: 1½ hours

You can serve this dish hot or cold. For variety, you might make this dish the night before a picnic. Let the cooked chicken marinate in the heated sauce overnight (in the refrigerator) and seal it in a plastic bowl. Try it.

to prepare

1
Remove the fat and the rear end from chicken. Wash the chicken.

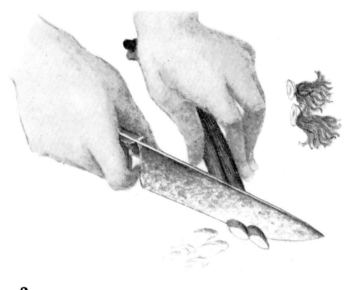

2
Cut the scallions into ¼-inch pieces.

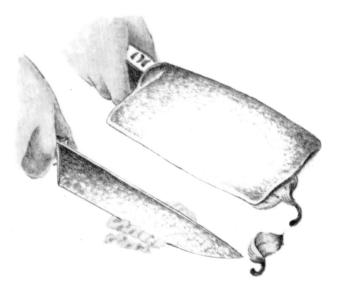

3
Crush the garlic and chop with a knife.

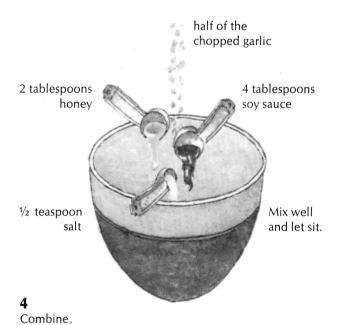

2 tablespoons honey

half of the chopped garlic

4 tablespoons soy sauce

½ teaspoon salt

Mix well and let sit.

4
Combine.

to cook

1
Put 3 quarts water in a large saucepan. Bring to a boil.

2
Put the whole chicken in the boiling water and cook for 15 minutes.

3
Turn off the flame and let the chicken sit in the hot water for 20 minutes. Take the chicken out of the pot and put it in the refrigerator for ½ hour.

4
Take the chicken out of the refrigerator and pull the meat off the bones. Cut the meat into 2-inch pieces. Arrange them on a plate.

5
Put 3 tablespoons oil in a small saucepan over a high flame.

6
When the oil is hot, reduce flame to medium and add the rest of the chopped garlic. Stir well for 10 seconds.

7
Add the scallions, ¼ teaspoon ground ginger, and ½ teaspoon crushed red pepper. Reduce to low flame and simmer for 3 minutes.

8
Add this hot sauce to the sauce you prepared in the mixing bowl. Mix the sauces together and pour over the chicken. Serve.

ROAST DUCK STUFFED WITH SCALLIONS

ingredients

1 5- to 7-pound duck
sugar
2 teaspoons salt
2 bunches scallions
water

Total prep & cooking time: 1¼ hours

If you want the duck less fatty, add 20 minutes to ½ hour at 350° to the cooking time.

to prepare

1
Defrost duck, if frozen. Cut off the rear end and the fat pouches (if any) just above the tail. Preheat oven to 400°. Wash the duck inside and out.

2
If you want really crisp skin, pump some air under the skin to separate it from the meat. Use one of those wine openers that has a needle and pumps air. (Don't do it if it's too much trouble.)

3
Coat the skin with sugar. Coat it about 2 grains thick (it's impossible but that's the idea!).

4
Sprinkle or shake 1 teaspoon salt evenly over the duck.

5
Cut the scallions into 1-inch pieces.

6
Mix the cut scallions with 1 cup water and 1 teaspoon salt.

7
Pour the scallion-water mixture into the duck. Hold rear up so the water won't come out.

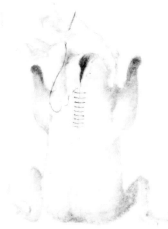

8
Sew up the duck with needle and thread. If no needle and thread, leave it open, but keep it tilted so the liquid won't pour out.

9
Put the duck on a rack.

to cook

1
Roast the duck for 45 minutes. Add 15 more minutes if duck is 7 pounds.

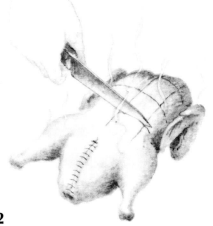

2
Turn oven up to 450° and brown duck for 8 minutes. Take out of oven. Use a sharp knife and cut off the skin. Cut the skin into 2-inch squares. (Do this only if you've pumped air between the skin and meat.)

3
Strip the meat off the duck bones. Arrange the meat on a plate and put the skin on top. Otherwise serve whole.

RED-COOKED DUCK

ingredients

1 5- to 7-pound duck (most likely
   it will be frozen)
2 onions
2 cups water
1 cup soy sauce
¼ cup dry sherry
2 tablespoons sugar
1 tablespoon cornstarch

Total prep & cooking time: 2¼ hours

A Very Important Note
When adding cornstarch or flour to thicken a gravy, the instructions will say sprinkle and stir. To avoid lumping, stir very rapidly, beating the mixture with a fork.

to prepare

1
Defrost and wash the duck. Cut off the rear end and the fat pouches (if any) just above the tail.

2
Peel 2 onions and stuff the duck with them.

to cook

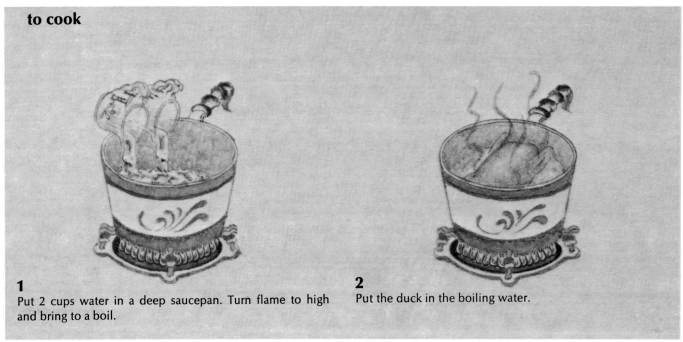

1
Put 2 cups water in a deep saucepan. Turn flame to high and bring to a boil.

2
Put the duck in the boiling water.

3
Add 1 cup soy sauce and ¼ cup dry sherry. Bring to a boil again.

4
Reduce flame to low, cover the pot, and simmer for 1 hour.

5
Turn the duck over.

6
Add 2 tablespoons sugar and stir into the sauce. Cover the pot and simmer for 1 hour more.

7
Take a cup of the sauce and put it in a small saucepan over a low flame.

8
Add 1 tablespoon cornstarch to the sauce and stir. When it's thick, put the gravy in a gravy dish.

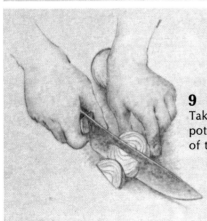

9
Take the duck out of the pot. Take the onions out of the duck.

10
Cut up the onions and add them to the gravy. Carve the duck and serve.

RED-COOKED CHICKEN

ingredients

½ broiling chicken
3 tablespoons oil
1 cup water
½ cup soy sauce
½ teaspoon salt
¼ teaspoon ground ginger
1 tablespoon sugar

Total prep & cooking time: 1 hour

to prepare

Wash the chicken and cut it apart. Or you can buy chicken parts already cut up.

to cook

1
Put 3 tablespoons oil in a deep sauce-pan. Turn flame to medium-high.

2
When the oil is hot, add the chicken. Cook for 5 minutes. Stir now and then to brown all parts of the chicken.

3
Add 1 cup water, ½ cup soy sauce, ½ teaspoon salt, ¼ teaspoon ground ginger. Bring the sauce to a boil.

4
After it boils, reduce flame to low, cover pan and simmer for 20 minutes.

5
Add 1 tablespoon sugar. Stir in well. Cover pan and simmer for 20 minutes. Serve hot or cold.

rice wine

Drinking wine with Chinese food has become popular in this country. If you like rice wine (sake), you might try the traditional Chinese way of drinking it. Rice wine is really smooth after heating. A good way to heat the wine is to fill a large saucepan with hot, but not boiling, water. Immerse the wine bottle in the hot water for about ten minutes—but make sure the bottle has been brought to room temperature before you immerse it. To guard against the bottle's cracking in the heat, you might put the bottle under the hot-water tap for a few minutes. Serve the warm wine with the meal.

If you have a favorite white wine, you should definitely use it for the Drunken Chicken dish on page 44. In general, you can substitute any table wine for the dry sherry that's suggested in my recipes. With Red-Cooked Duck or Red-Cooked Pork you can use your favorite red wine, or even a good cognac, instead of the dry sherry. It gives the meat and the sauce a deeper and mellower flavor.

from frying pan to serving platter

I like to empty the contents of a frying pan by scooping out a few spoonfuls, then tilting the pan and gently pouring out the remainder, gravy and all. Arrange the food, if necessary, with a spoon before serving.

cleaning pots and pans

There's a trick to cleaning pots and frying pans. The best time to clean them is when they are hot off the fire. For example, if you want to stir-fry two dishes for dinner, do the following: stir-fry the first one and empty the contents of the frying pan onto a serving platter. Then take the frying pan to the sink and rinse out with hot water, using the spatula to scrape off any particles stuck to the bottom of the pan. In about 10 seconds the pan will be clean. Then set it on a high flame to dry. As soon as it dries, you are ready to cook the next dish. Stir-frying is very quick, and if you have all your dishes prepared and cut, ready for stir-frying, you could cook one dish after the other practically without interruption.

to slice but Not to cut

The best way to slice meats or cut vegetables without cutting your fingers is to curl your fingertips slightly so that your fingernails dig into the meat, and your first knuckle is against the side of the knife or cleaver. The bigger the knife, the less chance you have of cutting yourself. Your knuckles will also serve as a guide for your knife in determining the thickness of the slice. Move your knuckles back ⅛ inch, then move the side of the knife against your knuckles. Press down to cut the meat, and you'll get a ⅛-inch-thick slice.

dried mushrooms

Use dried mushrooms in any dish that has a lot of sauce in it. They are particularly good when cooked with the sauce in White Water Fish. Soak five or six dried mushrooms in warm water for 15 minutes. Cut the mushrooms into strips, add to the sauce, and cook. Dried mushrooms will soak up the sauce, whereas canned mushrooms won't. You'll taste the difference.

sesame oil

You can use Oriental sesame oil for just about everything—but use it in moderation. For example, a few drops added to any soup brings out a delightful flavor. Add two or three drops to each bowl of soup as you serve. Add the sesame oil on top of the soup; don't put into the empty bowl. Add a few drops to your cooking oil when you cook vegetables, meat, or fish. Keep the sesame oil refrigerated and it will last for a long time; one bottle could last a year or two.

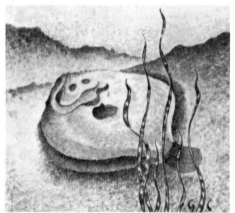

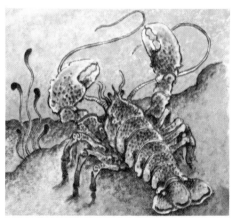

SEAFOOD

In Chinese cooking, fish are cooked whole and served whole for aesthetic reasons and also so that the guest of honor can have easy access to the best and most tender part of the fish.

The two pieces of meat tucked away in the cheeks of the fish, though small, are the sweetest and tenderest pieces of meat in any fish. If you've always been squeamish about fish heads, these choice pieces may change your mind.

Cooking times will vary depending on the sizes of the fish or shrimps. Small baby shrimps will only take about four minutes to cook thoroughly. Slightly larger ones will take six minutes, and big ones will take eight to ten minutes. In any case, the shrimps should be firm when you bite into them. If they are soft, then they are not cooked all the way through. If they are too hard and stringy, they are overcooked. Very large shrimps are sometimes tough —just because they *are* large and stringy—so we prefer to cook with tender baby shrimps—they are sweeter and more delicate in taste and better suited to sauces.

Seafood is economical because it's filling—the way we Chinese cook it. Most of my recipes are designed for *eaters* and ease in cooking. For example, all of my shrimp dishes call for one pound of shrimps. One pound of shrimps with peas, served with rice, is more than enough for two people. And there you have it: a good, simple, easy dinner.

You should vary the amount of shrimps according to the number of people you want to feed, and the amount they normally eat. Some people are not big eaters, and half a pound of shrimps with half a box of frozen peas will suffice for two. But that's up to you when you plan your menu. (See Menu Planning section, page 12.)

I usually like to cook too much of everything. I do it on purpose because I like leftovers. Leftovers are great for lunch or brunch, snacks, and, if you accumulate enough, another full meal. Leftovers are also great with leftover rice.

The basis for fried rice—and the un-Chinese chop suey —is the mixing of all the leftovers into one big dish. The only things you shouldn't put into fried rice are fish with bones and other obviously hazardous dishes. You should really bone everything first, including chicken.

Some dishes get better as leftovers. Red-Cooked Pork Shoulder, for instance. Keep the leftover pork refrigerated. When served hot, days later, it will taste even better.

I cook too much because I'm lazy. It's like cooking two meals with the effort of one. And what's nice about that is there's no loss of quality or taste.

Just a reminder: if you feel lazy but you want to feed two people, then just make one shrimp dish. But if you feel ambitious, make a fish as well, cut down on the quantity of shrimp, and make one other dish with vegetables in it. If you want to feed four adults who are big eaters, you should think in terms of ½ pound of shrimps or one whole fish, or ½ pound of fish fillet; ½ pound of pork; ½ pound of beef; and ½ pound of chicken or one chicken breast. That amount of meat and fish, plus whatever vegetables go with each dish, will be more than enough. With rice and a "house" soup, you'll probably have leftovers. You can feed four big eaters very economically.

When I say whole fish, I mean a whole fish, *cleaned, scaled, but not decapitated.* Recently friends of mine asked the fishmonger for a whole fish. He sold it to them whole and uncleaned. American fishmongers are used to cutting the heads off the fish as part of the cleaning process. When you ask for it whole, they might take that to mean uncleaned. Make sure they clean and scale the fish.

Another thing: people like sauce with their rice. Most of my dishes have plenty of sauce in them. But if you have a few young ones around, you might want to make more sauce. For friends who love sauce with their rice, I usually add a little more water mixed with cornstarch or flour— about ¼ cup of water at most. Experiment and work out the tastes that suit you.

Now a word about cornstarch *vs* flour: You use either one to thicken the sauce. If you want a clear sauce, use cornstarch. If you don't care, then use flour. For example, I'd use cornstarch for egg-drop soup because I want it looking translucent, so I can see the egg drops suspended throughout the soup. Neither flour nor cornstarch affects the taste of any dish—they are used primarily for aesthetic reasons.

STEAMED FLOUNDER (OR SEA BASS)

ingredients

1 fatty pork chop
4 scallions
1 pound flounder fillets
vegetable oil
½ cup chicken broth
1 teaspoon salt
1 teaspoon sugar
few shakes of pepper
¼ teaspoon ground ginger
2 tablespoons dry sherry

Total prep & cooking time: 25 minutes

to prepare

1
Slice the pork chop into thin strips.

2
Cut the scallions into 1-inch pieces.

3
Coat each piece of flounder with vegetable oil.

4
Put the flounder in an ovenproof serving plate. Lay the sliced pork over the fish fillets. Distribute the pork evenly among the fillets.

5
Pour in the ½ cup of chicken broth.

6
Sprinkle 1 teaspoon salt, 1 teaspoon sugar, and a few shakes of pepper over the fish and sprinkle with ¼ teaspoon ground ginger.

7
Distribute the cut scallions and add 2 tablespoons dry sherry.

to cook

1
Pour water into a large pan to a depth of 1 inch. Put a rack in the pan for the ovenproof platter to sit on.

2
Put the platter with the fish on the rack. Turn the flame to high. Bring the water to a boil.

3
When the water boils, cover the pan. Reduce flame to medium and steam the fish for 15 minutes. Serve in the platter.

LOBSTER CANTONESE

ingredients

1 1½-pound lobster
½ cup chicken broth
1 tablespoon soy sauce
1 tablespoon flour
¼ cup lobster juice or water
4 scallions
1 clove garlic (optional)
1 egg

¼ pound ground pork
½ teaspoon salt
½ teaspoon pepper
¼ cup vegetable oil

Total prep & cooking time: 30 minutes

to prepare

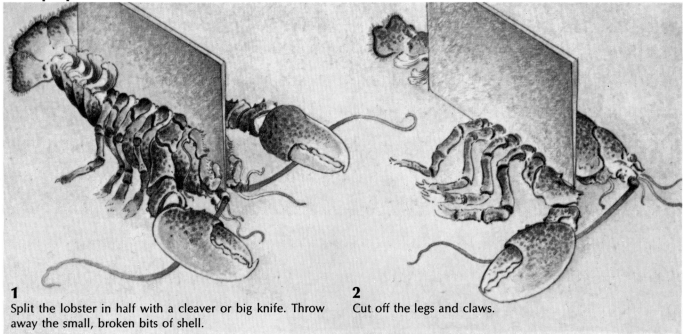

1
Split the lobster in half with a cleaver or big knife. Throw away the small, broken bits of shell.

2
Cut off the legs and claws.

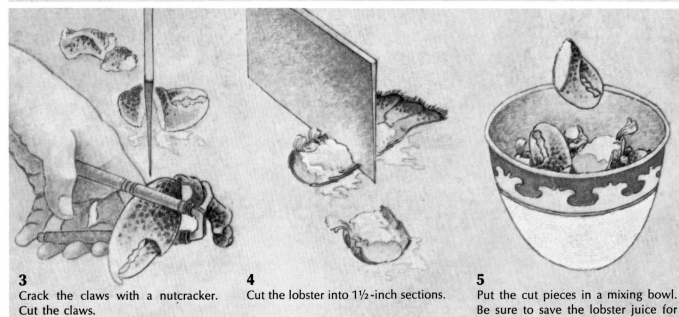

3
Crack the claws with a nutcracker. Cut the claws.

4
Cut the lobster into 1½-inch sections.

5
Put the cut pieces in a mixing bowl. Be sure to save the lobster juice for later use.

6
Have ½ cup chicken broth ready.

7
Mix 1 tablespoon soy sauce, 1 tablespoon flour, and ¼ cup lobster juice. If not enough juice, add water to make ¼ cup.

8
Cut 4 scallions into ¼-inch pieces. Dice 1 clove garlic (optional).

9
Beat 1 egg in a small mixing bowl.

10
In another mixing bowl, combine ¼ pound ground pork with the cut scallions, ¼ teaspoon salt, and ½ teaspoon pepper.

to cook

1
Put ¼ cup vegetable oil in a frying pan. Turn flame to high. Add the remaining ¼ teaspoon salt and the garlic.

2
When the oil is hot and garlic is sizzling, add the ground pork mixture. Stir for 1 minute.

3
Add the cut lobster and stir the whole thing for 1 minute.

Continued overleaf.

4
Add ½ cup chicken broth slowly, stirring as you do so—takes 30 seconds.

5
When the sauce boils, reduce flame to low, cover pan, and simmer for 3 minutes.

6
Remove cover, stir the lobster a few times. Cover again and simmer for 3 minutes more.

7
Add the soy sauce-flour-lobster-juice mixture. Stir well for 30 seconds.

8
Cover pan and simmer for 3 minutes. Stir now and again.

9
Remove cover and pour the beaten egg into the lobster sauce, stirring as you do so for 1 minute. Serve.

FRIED SHRIMPS

ingredients

1 pound raw shrimps (fresh or frozen)
2 eggs
¼ cup flour
2 tablespoons dry sherry
¼ teaspoon pepper
½ teaspoon salt
peanut oil for frying

Total prep & cooking time: 30 minutes

to prepare

1
Shell the shrimps and clean. Defrost if frozen.

2
Use a mixing bowl, crack 2 eggs into it and beat.

3
Slowly add ¼ cup flour to the eggs. Add 2 tablespoons dry sherry, ¼ teaspoon pepper, ½ teaspoon salt. Beat into a nice light batter.

to cook

4
Dip each shrimp into the batter; make sure all are completely covered.

1
Pour 1 inch (depth) oil into frying pan. Turn flame to medium high. Add shrimps, one at a time, to hot oil.

2
The shrimps are cooked when they are a nice, light brown. This takes about 3 to 4 minutes. Serve.

WHITE WATER FISH

ingredients

1 medium-sized sea bass or
  flounder (1 to 1½ pounds)
6 scallions
¼ cup vegetable oil
¾ cup soy sauce
1 small can mushrooms or 6 dried
  mushrooms
¼ teaspoon ground ginger
1 clove garlic, diced
1 tablespoon sugar

Total prep & cooking time: 30 minutes

This is a very gentle way of cooking any kind of fish. The technique keeps the fish moist and succulent. The similarity between this dish and White Cooked Chicken is not accidental.

to prepare

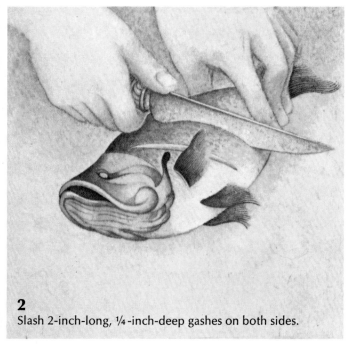

1
Wash the fish in cold water.

2
Slash 2-inch-long, ¼-inch-deep gashes on both sides.

3
Wash the scallions and cut.

to cook

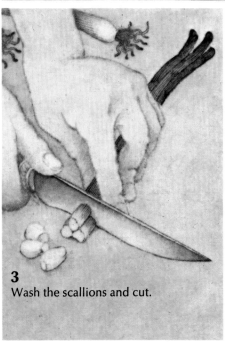

1
Fill a large pot with cold water, about ¾ full. Bring the water to a rapid boil.

2
Reduce flame to low. Put the fish in the pot. Don't let the water boil. Cook for 15 minutes.

3
Meanwhile, put ¼ cup vegetable oil and ¾ cup soy sauce in a frying pan. Place over medium fire and stir.

4
When the sauce begins to steam, add the mushrooms, ¼ teaspoon ground ginger, and 1 clove diced garlic. Stir for 2 minutes.

5
Add 1 tablespoon sugar. Stir the sugar into the sauce.

6
Reduce to a very, very low flame and simmer for 3 minutes. Stir now and again. Turn off flame.

7
By now your 15 minutes for the fish is up. Carefully take the fish out of the water and put it in the frying pan with the sauce.

8
Cook the fish in the sauce over a low flame for 5 minutes.

9
Add the cut scallions and stir into the sauce.

10
Carefully turn the fish over and cook for 3 minutes more. Serve.

RED-COOKED FISH

ingredients

1 2- to 3-pound fish (carp, perch, shad, mullet)
flour
3 scallions
peanut oil
½ cup soy sauce
3 tablespoons dry sherry
1 cup water
1 tablespoon sugar
2 teaspoons salt
¼ teaspoon ground ginger

Total prep & cooking time: 30 minutes

to prepare

1
Wash the fish.

2
Slash 2-inch-long, ¼-inch-deep gashes on both sides.

3
Coat the fish with a thin layer of flour.

4
Cut 3 scallions into 1-inch pieces.

to cook

1
Pour peanut oil 1 inch deep in a large frying pan. Turn flame to high.

2
When the oil is hot, put the fish in it. Cook for 1 minute. Turn the fish over and cook for 1 minute more.

3
Reduce fire to medium and cook for 3 minutes. Turn the fish over and cook for 3 minutes more.

4
Take the fish out and put it on a plate.

5
Pour off the frying oil, leaving about 1 tablespoon oil in the pan.

6
Add ½ cup soy sauce, 3 tablespoons dry sherry, and 1 cup water.

7
Put the fish in the pan again. Sprinkle 1 tablespoon sugar, 2 teaspoons salt, ¼ teaspoon ground ginger, and the cut scallions on top.

8
Turn flame to medium high. Cover pan and cook for 10 minutes. Serve the whole fish with the sauce.

PINEAPPLE FISH

ingredients

1½ pounds flounder fillets
3 tablespoons soy sauce
½ teaspoon salt
2 tablespoons dry sherry
2 eggs
2 tablespoons cornstarch
½ cup water
1 tablespoon sugar
1 small can diced pineapple
3 tablespoons vegetable oil

Total prep & cooking time: 30 minutes

to prepare

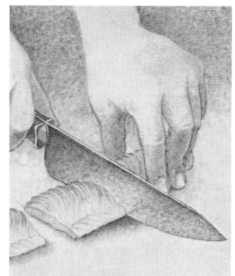

1
Cut the fillets into 2-inch pieces—or 3 pieces to each fillet.

2
In a mixing bowl, combine 3 tablespoons soy sauce, ½ teaspoon salt, and 2 tablespoons dry sherry. Marinate the fillets in this sauce for 15 minutes.

3
In another mixing bowl, combine ½ cup water, 1 tablespoon sugar, and the diced pineapple (drain the juice from the can). Set aside the pineapple sauce.

4
Meanwhile, in a third mixing bowl, beat 2 eggs. Add 2 tablespoons cornstarch, a little at a time, while beating.

5
Dip the cut fillets in the egg-cornstarch mixture. Put the fillets on a plate.

6
Add the leftover egg-cornstarch mixture to the pineapple sauce. Mix well.

to cook

1
Put 3 tablespoons vegetable oil in a frying pan. Turn heat to medium.

2
When the oil is hot, add the fish fillets. Fry for 2 minutes.

3
Turn the fillets over and fry for 2 minutes more. Take them out and arrange on a serving platter.

4
Put the pineapple sauce into a small saucepan. Bring the sauce to a boil. Stir.

5
When the sauce looks smooth and creamy, pour it over the fillets. Serve.

RED-COOKED BASS

ingredients

1 2-pound bass (freshwater or sea
   bass)
6 scallions
2 cloves garlic
4 tablespoons vegetable oil
¾ cup soy sauce
1 cup water
3 tablespoons dry sherry
¼ teaspoon ground ginger
1 tablespoon sugar
   flour (optional)

This is a good dish to add dried mushrooms to. Soak the dried mushrooms in warm water first (15 minutes) then let them cook in the sauce along with the fish.

Total prep & cooking time: 35 minutes

to prepare

1
Wash the fish.

2
Cut gashes 2 inches long and ¼ inch deep on both sides.

3
Cut the 6 scallions into 1-inch pieces.

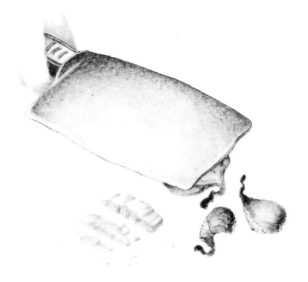

4
Finely chop 2 cloves garlic.

to cook

1
Put 4 tablespoons vegetable oil in a large frying pan. Turn flame to high.

2
When the oil is hot, add the diced garlic. Stir for 30 seconds.

3
Add ¾ cup soy sauce and 1 cup water. Bring to a boil.

4
When the sauce boils, reduce heat to medium, and put the fish in the pan.

5
Add 3 tablespoons dry sherry, and sprinkle with ¼ teaspoon ground ginger. Cover pan and cook for 5 minutes.

6
Turn the fish over and add 1 tablespoon sugar, stirring the sugar into the sauce. Cover and cook for 10 minutes.

7
Turn the fish over gently. Sprinkle the cut scallions over it. Cover the pan and cook for 7 minutes.

8
Serve the fish whole with the scallions and some of the sauce. If you like, you can add some flour to the remaining sauce in the pan to make a thick gravy.

SHRIMP WITH LOBSTER SAUCE

ingredients

1 pound shrimps (fresh or frozen)
2 scallions
½ teaspoon salt
1 clove garlic (optional)
1 egg
½ cup chicken broth
¼ pound ground pork

½ teaspoon pepper
½ tablespoon soy sauce
1 tablespoon flour
3 tablespoons oil

Total prep & cooking time: 40 minutes

This dish is called lobster sauce for two reasons: 1. It's the same sauce used for a lobster dish. 2. You're supposed to use some lobster meat from the head and base of the legs in the sauce, but that's impossible at home —it's only practical in restaurants.

to prepare

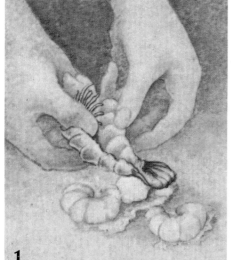

1
Shell the shrimps and put them in a bowl. Save the shrimp juice. If the shrimps are frozen, defrost them in a bowl. Save the juice.

2
Cut 2 scallions into ¼-inch pieces. Finely chop 1 clove garlic if you are using it.

3
Beat 1 egg in a small mixing bowl.

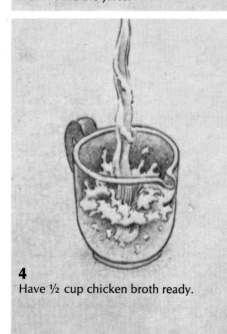

4
Have ½ cup chicken broth ready.

5
Mix ¼ pound ground pork with the cut scallions, ¼ teaspoon salt, and ½ teaspoon pepper.

6
Mix ½ tablespoon soy sauce with 1 tablespoon flour, and ¼ cup shrimp juice. Use water if you don't have any shrimp juice.

to cook

1
Put 3 tablespoons oil in a frying pan. Add the optional diced garlic and ¼ teaspoon salt. Turn flame to high. Stir.

2
When the garlic sizzles in the hot oil, add the ground pork mixture. Stir well for 1 minute.

3
Add the shrimps and stir for 30 seconds.

4
Add ½ cup chicken broth slowly, stirring as you do so. Take about a minute to do this.

5
When the sauce boils, reduce flame to low. Cover the pan and simmer for 4 minutes.

6
Remove cover; stir the shrimps a few times. Cover the pan and simmer for 3 minutes.

7
Add the soy sauce-flour-shrimp juice mixture and stir for 10 seconds. Cover pan and simmer for 3 minutes more.

8
Pour the beaten egg into the pan. Stir well for 1 minute. Take the pan off the heat. Serve.

SHRIMPS WITH PEAS

ingredients

1 pound raw shrimps (fresh or frozen)
2 scallions
1 package frozen peas (or 2 pounds fresh peas in the pod)
3 tablespoons oil
1 teaspoon salt
¼ teaspoon pepper
3 tablespoons dry sherry
1 tablespoon flour

A 1- minute cooking time doesn't sound like much, but it's a long time when you are cooking over a high flame. Just count to 60 as you are stirring. Don't rush yourself, a minute is a long time.

Total prep & cooking time: 20 minutes

to prepare

1
Shell the shrimps and clean. Defrost if frozen.

2
Cut the scallions into ¼ -inch pieces.

3
Shell the peas, if fresh. Defrost if frozen.

4
Put 3 tablespoons oil in frying pan.

to cook

1
Heat the oil over a high flame. When the oil is hot, add the cut scallions. Stir for 30 seconds.

2
Add the shrimps. Stir the shrimps so they cook evenly. Stir for 1 minute.

3
Add 1 teaspoon salt and ¼ teaspoon pepper. Stir for 1 minute.

4
Add 3 tablespoons dry sherry. Stir for 1 minute.

5
Add the peas. Stir for 1 minute.

6
Add 1 tablespoon flour. Stir a few times. Cook for 2 minutes, stirring now and then. Serve.

SWEET-AND-SOUR FISH

ingredients

1½ pounds flounder fillets
4 tablespoons cornstarch
1 small can diced pineapple
4 tablespoons catsup
4 tablespoons honey
6 tablespoons soy sauce
3 tablespoons dry sherry
⅓ cup vinegar
¼ cup water
¼ cup vegetable oil

Total prep & cooking time: 25 minutes

to prepare

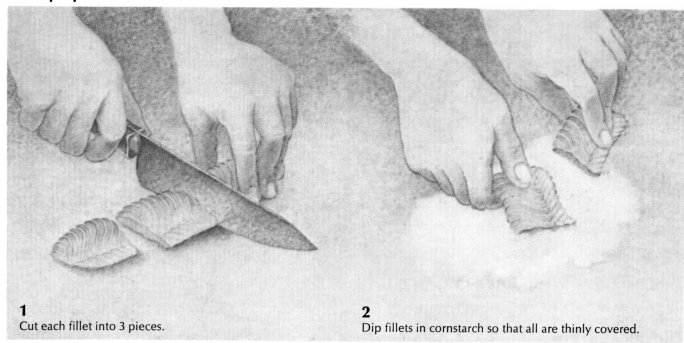

1
Cut each fillet into 3 pieces.

2
Dip fillets in cornstarch so that all are thinly covered.

diced pineapple
(drained)

⅓ cup
vinegar

3 tablespoons
dry sherry

¼ cup
water

2 tablespoons
cornstarch

6 tablespoons
soy sauce

4 tablespoons
catsup

4 tablespoons
honey

3
Mix well:

to cook

1
Put ¼ cup oil in a large frying pan. Turn flame to high.

2
When the oil is hot, reduce flame to medium. Add the fillets. Cook for 1 minute.

3
Turn the fish over and cook for 1 minute more. If your frying pan doesn't hold all the fish at once, you'll have to do this twice to cook it all.

4
Take the fish out and leave in a large plate.

5
Add the pineapple sauce to the frying pan. Turn flame to high. Stir.

6
When the sauce starts to bubble, reduce flame to medium low. Stir until the sauce is hot and smooth-looking.

7
Return the fish to the pan. Make sure the pieces are evenly distributed throughout the sauce. Spoon sauce over fillets so that all are covered with sauce.

8
Cover the pan and simmer for 3 minutes over low flame. Don't stir. Serve.

CRABMEAT WITH EGGS

ingredients

1 cup crabmeat (fresh or canned)
4 eggs
2 scallions
2 tablespoons vegetable oil
salt
pepper

Total prep & cooking time: 15 minutes

This dish is great for a late Sunday breakfast. Note: if you buy the canned crabmeat, usually it comes packed in salt water. In which case you needn't add any salt to the eggs.

to prepare

1
Remove any shell and tendons from the crabmeat; flake meat into small pieces.

2
Beat 4 eggs lightly as for scrambled eggs.

3
Cut the scallions into ¼-inch pieces.

4
Put 2 tablespoons vegetable oil in a frying pan.

to cook

1
Heat the oil over a high flame.

2
When the oil is hot, add the cut scallions. Stir for 30 seconds.

3
Add the crabmeat and stir for 3 minutes.

4
Pour the eggs over the crabmeat. Stir as you would scrambled eggs.

5
As you stir the eggs, add salt and pepper to taste. Take the pan off the heat, and serve.

SHRIMPS IN HOT SAUCE

ingredients

1 pound raw shrimps (fresh or frozen)
4 tablespoons catsup
6 tablespoons dry sherry
1 fresh hot pepper, red or green (use less if you want the dish less hot), or ½ teaspoon crushed red pepper

1 tablespoon flour
1 teaspoon sugar
3 tablespoons oil
½ teaspoon salt

Total prep & cooking time: 30 minutes

to prepare

1
Shell the shrimps and clean. Defrost if frozen. Dice the hot pepper.

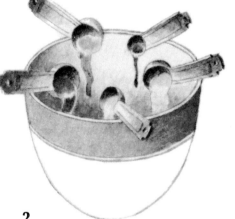

2
Mix 4 tablespoons catsup, 6 tablespoons dry sherry, the hot pepper, diced (or ½ teaspoon crushed red pepper), 1 tablespoon flour, and 1 teaspoon sugar.

to cook

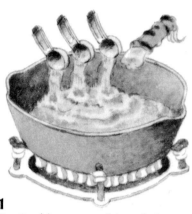

1
Put 3 tablespoons oil in a frying pan. Turn flame to high.

2
When the oil is hot, add the shrimps. Stir for 1 minute.

3
Add ½ teaspoon salt. Stir for 2 minutes.

4
Add the hot sauce you've mixed and stir for 2 minutes—or longer if the shrimps are big. Serve.

how to take a fish out of the frying pan

Pick up the frying pan. Place your spatula under the fish; tilt the pan to pour out the sauce. As you are pouring the sauce into the serving platter, hold the fish in the pan with the spatula. When some of the sauce is in the serving platter, let the fish gently slide down the frying pan, using your spatula as a guide. As the fish starts to slide, keep the frying pan as close to the serving platter as possible. Now, both of your hands should be in motion simultaneously. That is, guide the fish down with your spatula while lifting the frying pan up and away, in a sort of arch.

what to do with leftovers

Don't throw away leftovers. Once the food is cooked, it'll keep in the refrigerator for three days at least. I usually cook too much rice on purpose just so I can make fried rice with leftovers. You can make homemade fried rice with any dish or combination of dishes you like. There are just two things you shouldn't do: don't use fish with bones in it, or chicken with bones, or any sweet leftover dish. Sweet dishes should not be mixed with any other dish but another sweet dish.

here's how to make fried rice with your leftovers

You should have at least 6 tablespoons of leftovers. That could be as little as 3 tablespoons from 2 dishes or 2 table-spoons from 3 dishes. So don't throw away any little bit. We never waste food—every little bit can be used for fried rice. You should have at least 2 to 3 cups of leftover rice. If you've left the rice in the pot and placed it in the re-frigerator, as I do, then the rice will be one solid hunk after a day or two. Take the cold rice out and crumble it with your hands.

As a general rule, you should have a minimum of 6 tablespoons of leftover food to every 2 to 3 cups of left-over rice. More of everything is great, but that should be the minimum ratio. You'll also need an egg. Beat 1 egg for every 2 to 3 cups of rice. Use two eggs at most. You may need some soy sauce and water, too.

to cook

1
Put your leftover food in the frying pan and heat over low flame. Stir now and then.

2
When the food looks warm, or the sauce has melted or is steaming, add the leftover rice. Turn flame to medium. Stir now and then.

3
If the mixture looks too dry, add 1 tablespoon soy sauce and ¼ cup water. Stir well for 2 minutes.

4
Add the beaten egg slowly, stirring as you do so. Mix well until everything is hot. If you like dark fried rice, add more soy sauce. Serve.

Fried rice with leftovers is a traditional Chinese dish which could be a good side dish for families with children. Homemade fried rice will go well with hamburgers, hot dogs, or any leftover roast. It makes a good treat for the kids, especially if you had a "Chinese food party" the night before. The dish will only take about 5 to 10 minutes to make.

leftover shrimps

Shrimps are especially good for homemade fried rice. You can combine leftover shrimps with any kind of leftovers—pork, chicken, or beef. They even go well with sweet dishes. A few leftover shrimps, as few as two or three, along with other leftovers, would be a great addition to your home-made fried rice.

suggestions

For a family with children, the ground beef dishes in the next section are ideal for winter weekends. Ground Beef with Onions, Tomatoes, and Green Peppers served over rice is a favorite with the young, especially if you make more gravy with the dish (just add more water as you add the soy sauce). This dish, along with 1½ cups of uncooked rice, will ultimately serve three teen-aged kids. It'll be a hot lunch that they'll talk about.

If you are making curry dishes, one word of caution about the different brands of curry powder. The kind I prefer are the mild, domestic brands, not the really hot Indian curries. If you do like the hot Indian curry, I'd sug-gest you cut the amount in half—that is, unless you like things really hot. If your family likes hot dishes, then the Ground Beef with Hot Sausage Sauce would be a special treat on cold Saturday afternoons. Served over rice, these dishes are more interesting than hamburger, and possibly less expensive, too. This is a good way to vary your week-end routine and to expose your family to new and dif-ferent foods.

BEEF

The Chinese usually don't cook with ground beef, but I've taken the liberty of making things a little easier for the person in a hurry. To slice beef into thin strips is time-consuming and sometimes a deterrent to cooking dinner for yourself. It's no fun to cook for yourself (if you are single, that is), but it's a lot better than eating out all the time. Ground beef is cheap and easy to cook. Essentially, what I've done is saved you the trouble of slicing the beef by converting a number of sliced beef dishes to ground beef dishes.

Serving a beef dish (or pork or chicken) over rice or noodles is one of the oldest ways of serving a complete meal. Chinese peasants invented noodles thousands of years ago, and Marco Polo brought them back to Italy. Now even Simon and Garfunkel sing about them ("Eating Chow Fun in Chinatown"). Chow Fun is a broad, flat, pasty noodle. Now it's your turn to try it.

The key concept in Chinese food is the sauce. No matter where you are in China, almost all of the dishes will be cooked in a sauce—it's hard to think of an exception. Most sauces are designed to complement the meat or vegetables in the dish. Beef has a unique and rather strong flavor, so the sauces can be quite strong to match it. (In Chinese cooking, we seldom use side dishes of mustard or duck sauce. This habit came about through the Americanization of the Chinese restaurant. The authentic duck sauce should be used for Peking Duck, and the sweet restaurant version and the mustard should be used only with certain types of dumplings. More about that later.)

Northern Chinese like to make thick, heavy sauces—sauces that are full-bodied and substantial. I suspect that the reason for this is the long, cold winters. Heavy meat sauces and hot-and-sour soup (a very substantial soup with about six ingredients in it, and not in this book because the ingredients are hard to get) will help fight off the cold. The body burns up more energy, so it needs more fuel.

In Szechuan cooking (that's the Wild West of China) everything is hot. I remember going with my mother to a restaurant somewhere in Szechuan Province and eating the hottest dish of noodles I had ever had in my young life. She simply smiled and said, "Well, they are famous for their hot sauces." Szechuan is really like our West, especially the mountainous sections. I suspect the reasons why Szechuan has such hot food are one, they grow a particularly hot peppercorn in that region, and two, the climate. Eating hot food helps you perspire, and perspiration brings down the body temperature; therefore, eating hot, spicy foods cools off the body. Hot Mexican food is another example. The body somehow craves it in that climate. So, should you ever visit Szechuan, eat what they are famous for and do it with a smile. It's good for you and will make your visit much more pleasant.

In southern China (which Cantonese cooking exemplifies) there's a sort of mixture of light and heavy sauces, and a few hot dishes. By a light sauce I mean the sauce in such dishes as White Water Fish and White-Cooked Chicken. You couldn't get lighter than that. Sometimes White-Cooked Chicken is served with a small plate of salt and pepper, mixed together, and that's it. Very light. It's great to eat that dish in that particular manner on a warm summer's night out in the back yard (with your fingers).

Among the few hot Cantonese dishes, the most notable is curry. Because the summers are very hot down south, the Cantonese like to have some hot dishes when needed, for the same reason that everything is hot in Szechuan. That's why curried beef and curried chicken are listed in most Cantonese restaurants. Practically everything else is mild and light.

But what has the hot mustard got to do with Cantonese cooking? Hot mustard, duck sauces, hot pepper sauce, vinegar, and soy-sauce vinegar are used most extensively with Chinese dumplings, or *dim sum*. There are about thirty varieties of Cantonese or southern dumplings, and about ten to fifteen northern dumplings. There are about fifty rather common dumplings that you can order or make, and quite a number of esoteric ones. But everyone knows about the egg roll. You can eat the egg roll with a number of sauces, even a mixture of them. For example, you can mix some vinegar with a drop or two of hot sauce and dip the egg roll in it; or dip it in vinegar and then in mustard; or mix the mustard with the duck sauce and dip it in that; or just use plain old soy-sauce vinegar.

BEEF WITH TOMATOES AND GREEN PEPPERS

ingredients

1 pound flank steak
3 medium-sized tomatoes
2 green peppers
2 medium-sized onions
1 teaspoon cornstarch
½ cup water
1 tablespoon sugar
½ cup soy sauce
¼ cup vegetable oil

Total prep & cooking time: 30 minutes

This dish will feed two adults and two children. It's a big dish. Usually, ½ pound of flank steak will be enough for two people. You can't buy a ½ pound piece, they usually come in 1 pound or larger pieces. Cut it down the middle, lengthwise, and then slice into thin pieces.

to prepare

1
Slice the flank steak into pieces, about ⅛-inch thick and 2 inches long. The meat is easier to slice if it's partially frozen.

2
Cut tomatoes into sections.

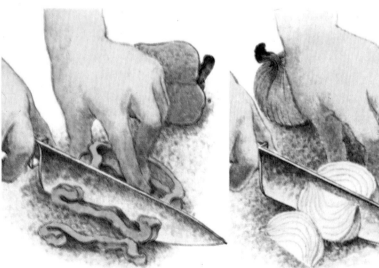

3
Thinly slice green peppers.

4
Cut onions into sections.

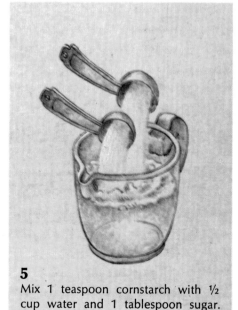

5
Mix 1 teaspoon cornstarch with ½ cup water and 1 tablespoon sugar. Have ½ cup soy sauce ready.

to cook

1
Put ¼ cup vegetable oil in a frying pan. Turn flame to medium-high.

2
When the oil is hot, add the onions and green peppers. Stir for 2 minutes.

3
Add the flank steak. Stir for 1 minute.

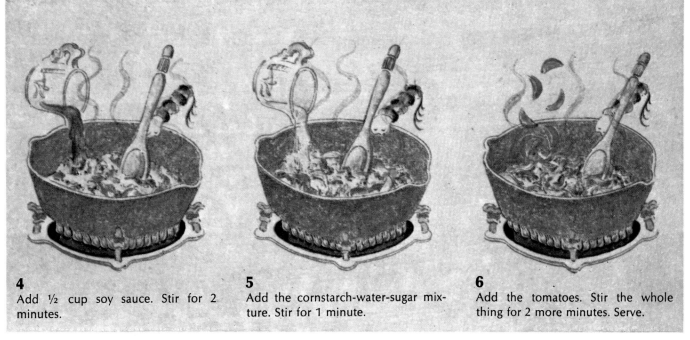

4
Add ½ cup soy sauce. Stir for 2 minutes.

5
Add the cornstarch-water-sugar mixture. Stir for 1 minute.

6
Add the tomatoes. Stir the whole thing for 2 more minutes. Serve.

RED-COOKED BEEF STEW

ingredients

1 pound stew beef
4 medium-sized onions
3 tablespoons dry sherry
4 tablespoons soy sauce
2 tablespoons honey
1 cup water
2 tablespoons oil

Total prep & cooking time: 70 minutes

to prepare

1
Cut the stew beef into 1-inch cubes.

2
Cut the onions into sections.

3 tablespoons
dry sherry

2 tablespoons
honey

4 tablespoons
soy sauce

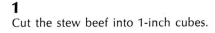

3
Mix well.

4
Have 1 cup water ready.

to cook

1
Put 2 tablespoons oil in a frying pan.
Turn flame to medium-high.

2
When the oil is hot, add the beef.
Turn the meat a few times to brown
all sides—takes about 3 to 4 minutes.

3
Add the soy sauce-honey-sherry mixture. Stir for 2 minutes.

4
Add 1 cup cold water. Bring to a boil.

5
Once it boils, turn flame to medium-
low and cover pan. Let cook for 20
minutes, stirring every 5 minutes.

6
Reduce flame to low and add onions.
Cover pan and simmer for 25 min-
utes, stirring now and then. Serve.

HOT SPICED BARBECUED BEEF

ingredients

1 pound sirloin steak
4 tablespoons soy sauce
2 tablespoons honey
¼ teaspoon salt
¼ teaspoon ground ginger
½ teaspoon crushed red pepper
3 scallions
1 clove garlic
2 tablespoons peanut oil

This dish is good for your outdoor charcoal broiler. The cooking time should be about the same depending on the heat from the coals.

Total prep & cooking time: 25 minutes

to prepare

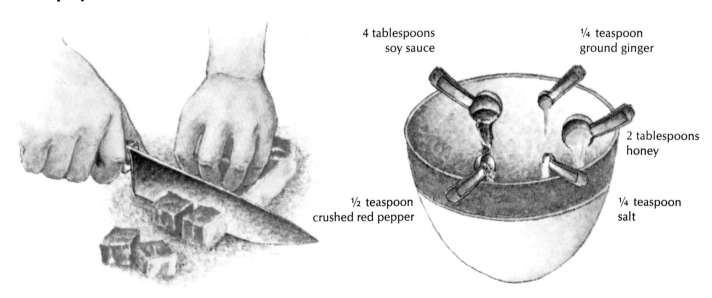

4 tablespoons soy sauce

¼ teaspoon ground ginger

2 tablespoons honey

½ teaspoon crushed red pepper

¼ teaspoon salt

1
Cut the sirloin steak into 1-inch cubes.

2
Mix well.

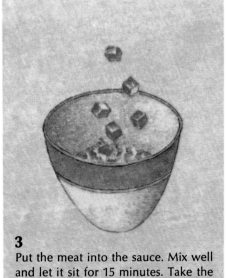

3
Put the meat into the sauce. Mix well and let it sit for 15 minutes. Take the meat cubes out of the sauce and arrange them on a broiling pan. Save the sauce.

4
Cut the scallions into ¼-inch pieces.

5
Crush the garlic and chop with a knife.

to cook

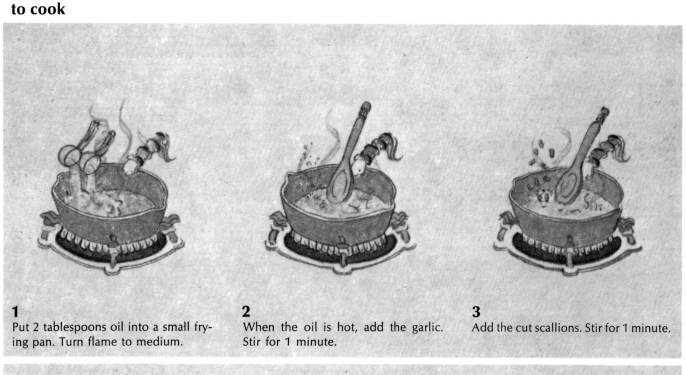

1
Put 2 tablespoons oil into a small frying pan. Turn flame to medium.

2
When the oil is hot, add the garlic. Stir for 1 minute.

3
Add the cut scallions. Stir for 1 minute.

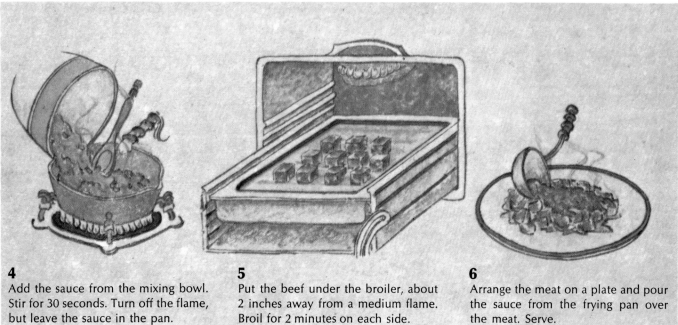

4
Add the sauce from the mixing bowl. Stir for 30 seconds. Turn off the flame, but leave the sauce in the pan.

5
Put the beef under the broiler, about 2 inches away from a medium flame. Broil for 2 minutes on each side.

6
Arrange the meat on a plate and pour the sauce from the frying pan over the meat. Serve.

BEEF WITH BROCCOLI

ingredients

½ pound flank steak
2 large stalks broccoli
3 tablespoons peanut oil
4 tablespoons soy sauce
1 tablespoon sugar
¼ teaspoon ground ginger
2 scallions
½ cup water
2 tablespoons flour

Total prep & cooking time: 30 minutes

Flank steaks usually come in 1-pound slabs or larger. Cut the steak down the middle, lengthwise, and then slice it into thin pieces. Freeze the other half for the next time. Or if you want to feed a family of four, use the whole pound and double the rest of the ingredients. If you can't get flank steak, try a round steak.

to prepare

1
Wash the broccoli under cold water.

2
Cut the heads of the broccoli from the stems and cut the big heads in half.

3
Slice the flank steak into thin strips 3 inches long.

4
Cut the scallions into ¼-inch lengths; have the other ingredients ready.

to cook

1
Heat 2 tablespoons of the peanut oil in a pan over a medium-high flame.

2
When the oil is hot, stir-fry the broccoli for 3 minutes. Put the broccoli on a plate and have it handy for cooking again.

3
Add 1 tablespoon oil to the pan, wait a few seconds, and add the flank steak. Stir-fry for 2 minutes.

4
Add 4 tablespoons soy sauce. Stir for 1 minute.

5
Sprinkle 1 tablespoon sugar over the beef, stir a few times and add the ¼-teaspoon ground ginger. Stir for 10 seconds.

6
Add the scallions and stir for 1 minute.

7
Return the broccoli to the pan and stir for 1 minute.

8
Add ¼ to ½ cup water to make more sauce and stir well for 20 seconds. Sprinkle 1 to 2 tablespoons flour in to thicken sauce. Stir well for 20 seconds. Serve.

BEEF WITH ASPARAGUS

ingredients

½ pound flank steak
½ pound fresh asparagus
2 tablespoons soy sauce
1 tablespoon dry sherry
2 tablespoons honey
¼ teaspoon salt
1 teaspoon flour
2 scallions
4 tablespoons oil

Total prep & cooking time: 20 minutes

to prepare

1
Slice the flank steak into thin slices.

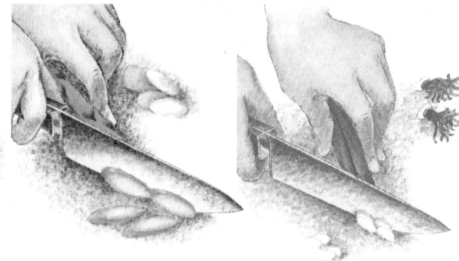

2
Wash the asparagus. Cut off the tough ends. Slice the asparagus with the crosscut.

3
Cut the scallions into ¼-inch pieces.

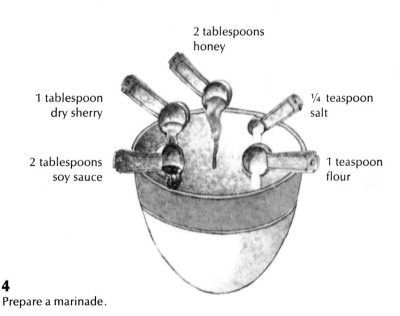

2 tablespoons honey

1 tablespoon dry sherry

¼ teaspoon salt

2 tablespoons soy sauce

1 teaspoon flour

4
Prepare a marinade.

5
Mix the sliced flank steak into the marinade. Let it sit for 10 minutes.

to cook

1
Add 2 tablespoons oil to a frying pan. Use high flame.

2
When the oil is hot, reduce to medium flame, and add the sliced asparagus. Stir for 2 minutes.

3
Take the asparagus out and set aside on a plate.

4
Add 2 more tablespoons oil to the frying pan again, keeping on medium flame.

5
When the oil is hot, add the marinated meat. Stir for 1 minute.

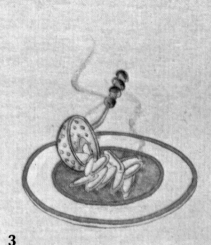

6
Return the asparagus to pan. Also add the cut-up scallions. Stir for 2 minutes. Remove from heat, but keep stirring for 1 more minute. Serve.

CURRIED BEEF STEW

ingredients

2 pounds stew beef
3 to 4 medium-sized onions
2 baking potatoes
4 tablespoons curry powder
2 cups water
3 tablespoons oil
1 teaspoon salt
2 tablespoons flour

Total prep & cooking time: 1 hour

to prepare

1

Cut the stew beef into 1-inch cubes.

2

Cut the onions into sections.

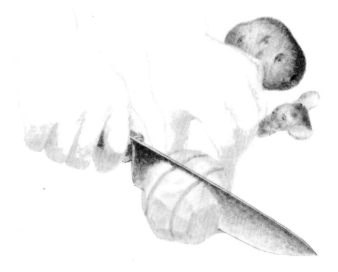

3

Wash and peel the potatoes. Cut each potato into 6 sections.

4

Put 4 tablespoons curry powder into a bowl. Add 2 cups of water. Blend with a spoon.

to cook

1
Put 3 tablespoons oil into stew pot. Place over high flame.

2
Put meat into pot. Stir for 2 minutes.

3
Add the curry powder-water mixture. Bring to a boil.

4
After it boils, reduce flame to low. Cover pot and cook for 10 minutes.

5
Add the potatoes. Cover pot and simmer for 20 minutes. Stir once or twice after 10 minutes.

6
Add the onions and 1 teaspoon salt. Cover pot and simmer for 10 minutes.

7
Add 2 tablespoons flour to thicken the sauce—more if you like a thick sauce. Stir as you add the flour.

8
The stew is cooked when the potatoes break apart with the touch of a fork. Serve.

GROUND BEEF WITH HOT SAUSAGE SAUCE

ingredients

½ pound ground beef
2 links hot Italian sausage or
   ½ pound ground pork and
   ½ teaspoon crushed red pepper
4 tablespoons soy sauce
2 tablespoons honey
2 tablespoons dry sherry
4 tablespoons water
2 tablespoons flour
1 large onion

Total prep & cooking time: 40 minutes

to prepare

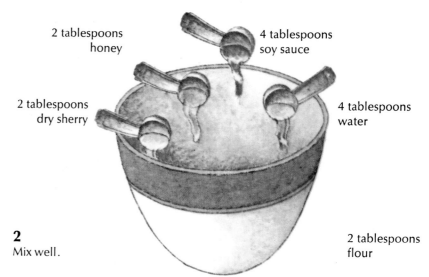

2 tablespoons honey

4 tablespoons soy sauce

2 tablespoons dry sherry

4 tablespoons water

2 tablespoons flour

1
Slice open 2 links hot sausage. Peel off the skin and discard. Or mix the ground pork with ½ teaspoon crushed red pepper.

2
Mix well.

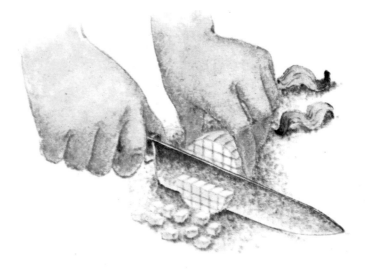

3
Add the ground beef to the sauce. Mix the beef and the sauce together with your fingers.

4
Dice the onion.

to cook

1
Put the peeled sausages or the ground pork into the frying pan. Turn flame to medium.

2
Stir the sausage or pork with a fork for 3 minutes. Don't let the meat stick to the bottom of the pan.

3
Add the ground beef-sauce mixture. Stir-cook for 5 minutes over medium-low flame.

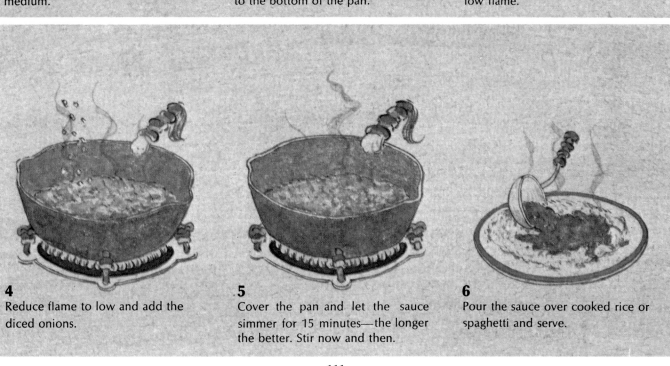

4
Reduce flame to low and add the diced onions.

5
Cover the pan and let the sauce simmer for 15 minutes—the longer the better. Stir now and then.

6
Pour the sauce over cooked rice or spaghetti and serve.

BEEF WITH SCALLIONS

ingredients

½ pound beef fillet (or flank steak)
6 scallions
5 tablespoons oil
1 tablespoon dry sherry
2 tablespoons soy sauce
¼ teaspoon salt
1 teaspoon sugar
1 teaspoon flour
pinch of ground ginger
⅛ teaspoon pepper

Total prep & cooking time: 15-20 minutes

to prepare

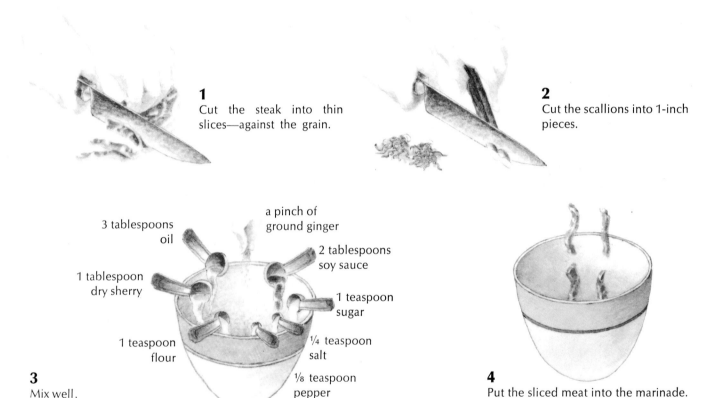

1
Cut the steak into thin slices—against the grain.

2
Cut the scallions into 1-inch pieces.

3 tablespoons oil

a pinch of ground ginger

2 tablespoons soy sauce

1 tablespoon dry sherry

1 teaspoon sugar

1 teaspoon flour

¼ teaspoon salt

⅛ teaspoon pepper

3
Mix well.

4
Put the sliced meat into the marinade. Mix well and let it sit for 10 minutes.

to cook

1
Put 2 tablespoons oil into a frying pan. Heat over medium-high flame. Add the scallions and stir rapidly for 2 minutes.

2
Add the marinated meat and its marinade. Stir-cook for 2 to 3 minutes. Serve.

QUICK CURRIED BEEF WITH ONIONS

ingredients

1 pound flank steak
2 medium-sized onions
2 tablespoons curry powder
½ cup water
1 tablespoon flour
½ teaspoon salt
3 tablespoons oil

Total prep & cooking time: 15 minutes

to prepare

1
Slice the flank steak into thin strips 2 inches long.

2
Cut the onions into sections.

3
Mix 2 tablespoons curry powder with ½ cup water.

4
Have 1 tablespoon flour and ½ teaspoon salt ready.

to cook

1
Add 3 tablespoons oil to a frying pan. Put over a medium-high flame. Add the flank steak and stir for 2 minutes.

2
Add the curry powder-water mixture. Stir for 2 minutes.

3
Add the cut onions. Stir a few times.

4
Add 1 tablespoon flour and ½ teaspoon salt. Stir for 3 minutes. Serve.

GROUND BEEF WITH ONIONS, TOMATOES, AND GREEN PEPPERS

ingredients

½ pound ground beef
1 large onion
2 small tomatoes
1 green pepper
4 tablespoons soy sauce
2 tablespoons honey
¼ teaspoon black pepper
2 tablespoons flour

Total prep & cooking time: 25 minutes

to prepare

1
Dice the onion.

2
Slice the green pepper.

3
Slice the tomatoes.

4
Mix 4 tablespoons soy sauce with 2 tablespoons honey, ¼ teaspoon black pepper, and 2 tablespoons flour.

to cook

1
Put the ground beef in the pan over a medium flame. Break it up with a fork. Cook for 5 minutes, stirring now and then.

2
Add the green pepper and stir for 1 minute.

3
Add the onions and stir for 1 minute.

4
Add the soy sauce-honey mixture and stir for 1 minute.

5
Add the tomatoes and stir for 1 minute.

6
Reduce to low flame and simmer for 3 minutes, stirring a few times. Serve the meat sauce over cooked rice or spaghetti.

BARBECUED BEEF

ingredients

1 pound sirloin steak
3 tablespoons honey
2 tablespoons soy sauce
1 clove garlic
¼ teaspoon salt

Total prep & cooking time: 20 minutes

You can make this dish in your charcoal broiler outdoors. The meat will cook in a minute or two if the coals are very hot.

to prepare

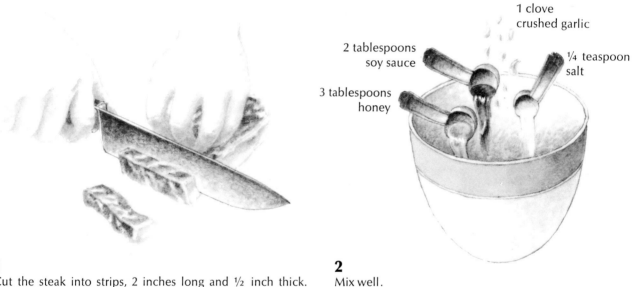

2 tablespoons
soy sauce

3 tablespoons
honey

1 clove
crushed garlic

¼ teaspoon
salt

1
Cut the steak into strips, 2 inches long and ½ inch thick. Cut against the grain.

2
Mix well.

to cook

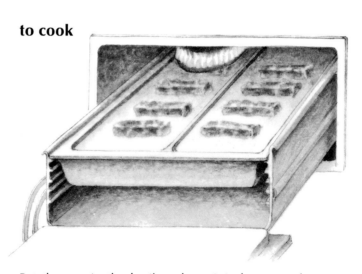

3
Add the meat to the marinade and mix well. Let it sit for 10 minutes. Arrange the meat in a pan for the broiler.

Put the pan in the broiler, about 2 inches away from a medium flame. Broil for 2 minutes. Take the pan out of the broiler. Turn the meat over. Put it back in the broiler for 2 minutes. Serve.

scallions (green onions)

For Chinese cooking, we like to use the whole thing, including the green part. So, whenever you see instructions for dicing or cutting scallions, use both the white and the green. Throw away the roots and any part (mostly the tips) of the green that looks withered or brownish. The smell of scallions being stir-fried is delightful, and it probably smells stronger than it tastes. The scallion appeals to both senses.

garlic

Garlic is usually considered a "strong" spice, and many Americans are reluctant to use it. Take heart, here's what happens to the garlic when prepared and cooked the Chinese way: when you crush it with the flat of your knife or cleaver, you squeeze some of the juice out. You've just taken some of the strength out of a clove of garlic. After dicing, the stir-frying in hot oil further diminishes it's strength. By the time you add and cook all the other ingredients, the garlic will long have lost it's "sting" and what remains is its delightfully unique flavor, a flavor which you'll probably be able to smell more than taste. The aroma of Chinese cooking should be as pleasant as the lush green of your fresh vegetables.

fresh vegetables

If you've never cooked vegetables the Chinese way, then you are in for a treat. Stir-frying vegetables take just a few minutes, and your vegetables will be a lush green. Most Americans are used to cooking the "life" and juices out of fresh vegetables, so much so that broccoli turns out to be limp and grayish green. When you cook Beef with Broccoli, you'll see that the broccoli will stay green, in fact, they'll look greener than before you cook them. If the broccoli turns brown or grayish or looks limp, then you know you've overcooked it. That holds for *any* fresh vegetables. A note about frozen vegetables: I don't like to use frozen vegetables, if I can get the same thing fresh, for this reason: the freezing process crystallizes the natural moisture between the fibers of the vegetables. When you defrost it, some of the crystallized moisture runs out, too, leaving the vegetable less juicy. But frozen vegetables are great when you can't get them fresh.

If you live in New York, Los Angeles, San Francisco, or Chicago, then you have access to stores which can provide you with fresh ginger, dried Chinese mushrooms, Oriental sesame oil, dried Szechuan peppers and so on. Not that you'd need these ingredients for this cookbook. But, in case you get the urge to try the real thing, here are two companies that will fill mail orders:

The Wing Fat Company
35 Mott Street
New York, N.Y. 10013

The Oriental Country Store
12 Mott Street
New York, N.Y. 10013

fresh ginger

Fresh ginger will keep in the refrigerator for two to three weeks; then it begins to get dried-out looking. Practically speaking, if you are going to use it while it's fresh, you should not order more than one or two pieces at a time. However, there are two satisfactory methods for keeping fresh ginger for months. One is to peel the ginger, cut it into half-inch chunks, put it in a jar, and pour dry sherry over to cover; cap the jar and store in the refrigerator, removing a piece or so to slice as needed. The other is, after peeling and slicing the same way, to put the ginger into a plastic storage container and keep in the freezer compartment of your refrigerator. For my recipes, slice ginger into two pieces about 1/8 inch thick, then cut into fine strips.

Use that amount of fresh ginger wherever you wish to substitute it for ground ginger in a recipe. If you like the ginger flavor, then slice more the next time.

old green beans

Green beans are one vegetable that I buy and keep in the refrigerator without worrying too much about their going stale. If your fresh green beans begin to look dry and shriveled (but not brown or moldy-looking) don't discard them. That's the time to cook them with ground pork. Try this—you'll be pleasantly surprised.

SOUPS AND VEGETABLES

The idea of making homemade soups with canned chicken broth is not my idea of "homemade." Chinese soups should be made from scratch with pure, fresh water. The flavoring of the soup should come from the ingredients that you add to it.

My grandmother didn't go to the corner store for beef or chicken broth—she used what was at hand. She would make her own beef broth from meat bones, leftover hunk of beef, or pieces of beef too tough for ingestion and digestion. The amount of broth would depend on the amount of scraps at hand. And, what's so hard about boiling a few pieces of beef to get some homemade broth? It's certainly more satisfying and much less expensive than the store-bought.

All of the soups in this book are what I call "table" soup or "house" soup. By that I mean the soups are easy to make, and they are completely homemade. (People have asked me why I don't use chicken broth to make egg-drop soup. Well, it seems kind of silly to first cook some pieces of chicken to make a broth, then use the broth to make the soup. And on top of that, add an egg! Egg-drop soup flavor should come from the egg, and nothing else.) These soups should be served with the rest of the meal—in fact, they should be considered as part of the meal. And you drink soup in lieu of tea, milk, Coke, or any other beverage that might interfere with the flavors of your dinner. The way to do it is to place a small soup bowl at each place setting. Then suggest that everyone drink soup as and when they feel like it (serving themselves, naturally). This is especially good when you serve a hot (spicy) dish. You'll

find that a bowl of warm soup will help to clear your palate, and take away some of the heat!

These are real soups, the way we used to make them. And they are very different from the usual restaurant soups. Restaurants add more stuff because you are paying for it. Besides, how could they justify charging all that money for a bowl of house soup?

In China and in certain Chinese restaurants in New York and San Francisco, you get house soup free with the meal. It's free because it is generally considered to be part of the meal. It's traditional.

The interesting thing about the whole soup thing is that restaurants will serve house soup only to Chinese patrons, and to no one else. I wonder what would happen if all patrons started to demand it as part of their meal?

There are many different types of Chinese vegetables; unfortunately, few are available in most local markets. But vegetables like broccoli, asparagus, tomatoes, onions, scallions and green peppers may be cooked the Chinese way with meats, chicken and fish. This ensures a substantially balanced diet and at the same time gives the vegetables some added flavor. My young daughter dislikes plain vegetables, but she does like them served the Chinese way —all mixed up with meat and sauce.

There are few strictly vegetable dishes in Chinese cuisine. For those of you who like vegetables, I've included a number of ways to cook one that's available throughout the U.S.—Chinese cabbage (also called celery cabbage). Chinese cabbage is a favorite in the Orient. The Koreans use it to make their famous *kim chee*.

BEAN SPROUTS WITH SOY SAUCE

ingredients

½ pound fresh bean sprouts
  (canned if fresh are not available)
2 tablespoons oil
½ teaspoon salt
3 tablespoons soy sauce

Total prep & cooking time: 10 minutes

to prepare

Soak the bean sprouts in water for a few minutes before cooking. Drain, but leave some moisture.

to cook

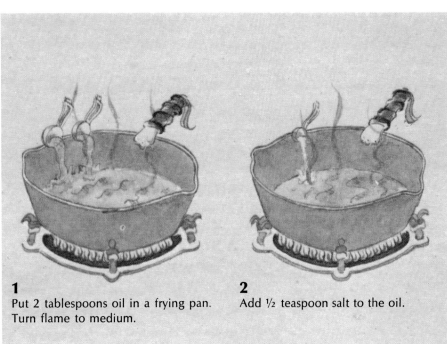

1
Put 2 tablespoons oil in a frying pan. Turn flame to medium.

2
Add ½ teaspoon salt to the oil.

3
Add the bean sprouts and stir-cook for 1 minute.

4
Add 3 tablespoons soy sauce. Stir for 2 minutes.

5
Reduce to low flame and stir-cook for 3 minutes. Serve.

COLD ASPARAGUS SALAD

ingredients

1 pound fresh asparagus
3 cups water
2 tablespoons soy sauce
2 tablespoons peanut oil
¼ cup white vinegar
pepper to taste

Total prep & cooking time: 30 minutes

This dish is good to take along on a picnic with any chicken dish. This and Chicken with Wine Sauce could make an ordinary picnic an extraordinary one.

to prepare

1
Wash the asparagus under cold running water.

2
Cut off the tough ends and discard. Slice the spears diagonally.

to cook

1
Bring 3 cups water to a rapid boil.

2
Add the cut asparagus. Bring the water to boil again. Boil the asparagus for 2 minutes.

3
Turn off the fire and take the asparagus out of the hot water with a slotted spoon. Put the asparagus in the refrigerator until cold.

4
Mix the cold asparagus with 2 tablespoons peanut oil, 2 tablespoons soy sauce, and ¼ cup vinegar. Add pepper to taste. Serve.

COLD (HOT) SESAME NOODLES

ingredients

2 tablespoons peanut butter
2 tablespoons peanut oil
½ teaspoon Oriental sesame oil
(if you can get it)
½ teaspoon crushed red pepper
(optional)
1½ quarts water
½ teaspoon salt
6 ounces fine egg noodles

Total prep & cooking time: 20 minutes

to prepare

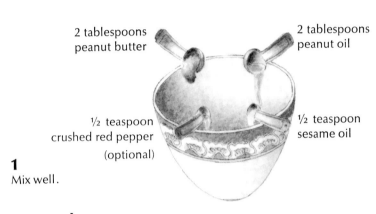

2 tablespoons
peanut butter

2 tablespoons
peanut oil

½ teaspoon
crushed red pepper
(optional)

½ teaspoon
sesame oil

1
Mix well.

2
Whip the peanut-butter mixture with a fork until it is loose enough to run off the fork.

to cook

1
Add 1½ quarts water to large saucepan. Bring water to a boil over a high flame.

2
Add ½ teaspoon salt and the egg noodles to the boiling water. Boil for 10 minutes.

3
Drain the noodles in a colander.

4
Mix the noodles with the peanut-butter sauce. Serve. If the dish is to be served cold, put it in the refrigerator to chill, then serve.

HOT-AND-SOUR COLD CABBAGE SALAD

ingredients

½ head Chinese cabbage (or
   celery cabbage)
3 tablespoons oil
1 teaspoon salt
⅓ cup white vinegar
½ teaspoon crushed red pepper
1 teaspoon sugar
1 tablespoon flour   Total prep & cooking time: 10 minutes

to prepare

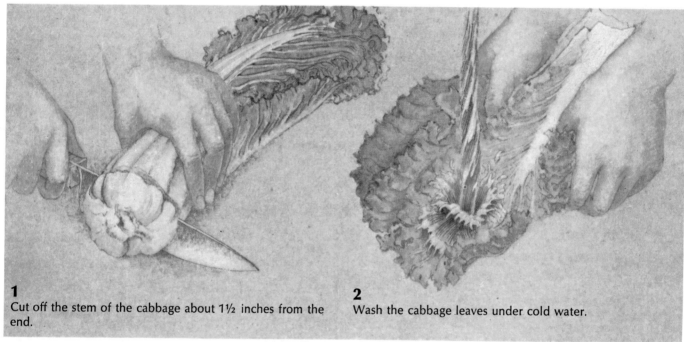

1
Cut off the stem of the cabbage about 1½ inches from the end.

2
Wash the cabbage leaves under cold water.

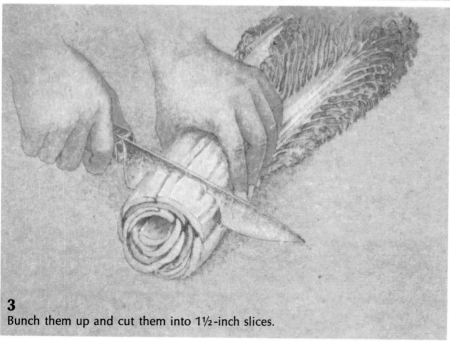

3
Bunch them up and cut them into 1½-inch slices.

4
Put 3 tablespoons oil in a frying pan.

to cook

1
Turn flame to high. When the oil is hot, add the cut cabbage. Stir for 1 minute.

2
Sprinkle 1 teaspoon salt over the cabbage. Stir for 10 seconds.

3
Add ⅓ cup vinegar and ½ teaspoon crushed red pepper. Stir-cook for 30 seconds and reduce flame to low.

4
Cover pan and simmer for 2 minutes.

5
Add 1 teaspoon sugar and stir for 10 seconds.

6
Add 1 tablespoon flour, a little at a time to thicken the sauce. Stir for 30 seconds. Dish may be served hot or cold.

SWEET-AND-SOUR CABBAGE

ingredients

½ head Chinese cabbage
   (or American cabbage)
3 tablespoons oil
1 teaspoon salt
⅓ cup white vinegar
2 tablespoons sugar
1 tablespoon flour

Total prep & cooking time: 10 minutes

to prepare (See page 122.)

to cook

1
Turn flame to high. When the oil is hot, add the cut cabbage. Stir for 1 minute.

2
Sprinkle 1 teaspoon salt over the cabbage. Stir for 30 seconds.

3
Add ⅓ cup vinegar. Stir for 30 seconds and reduce heat to low.

4
Cover the pan and simmer for 2 minutes.

5
Add 2 tablespoons sugar and stir for 20 seconds.

6
Add 1 tablespoon flour, a little at a time, to thicken the sauce. Stir for 30 seconds. Dish may be served hot or cold.

WATERCRESS AND CHICKEN GIBLET SOUP

ingredients

1 bunch watercress
chicken giblets and liver
    (the package from 1 chicken)
4 cups water
½ teaspoon salt
1 tablespoon soy sauce
1 egg

Total prep & cooking time: 40 minutes

to cook

to prepare

1
Wash the watercress and break off
and discard the hard stems.

2
Wash the liver and giblets.

1
Add 4 cups water to a large saucepan. Use high flame to bring water
to a boil.

2
Add the chicken giblets. Bring to a
boil again. Cover pot and reduce
flame to medium. Boil for 5 minutes.

3
Reduce flame to low and skim the fat
off the top of the water.

4
Add ½ teaspoon salt and 1 tablespoon soy sauce. Cover pot and simmer for 20 minutes.

5
Turn flame to high and bring to a
rapid boil. Add the watercress. Boil
rapidly for 2 minutes.

6
Pour the hot soup into a large bowl.
Immediately crack an egg into the
center of the soup. Serve.

CUCUMBER SOUP

ingredients

¼ cucumber
1 scallion
¼ pound ground pork
1 teaspoon cornstarch
1 tablespoon soy sauce
1 teaspoon dry sherry
4 cups water
½ teaspoon salt
pepper to taste

Total prep & cooking time: 20 minutes

to prepare

1
Mix ¼ pound ground pork with 1 teaspoon cornstarch, 1 tablespoon soy sauce, and 1 teaspoon dry sherry.

2
Peel cucumber if outside has been waxed. Otherwise, leave skin on. Slice the cucumber into thin slices.

3
Chop the scallion.

to cook

1
Put 4 cups water into a saucepan. Bring the water to a boil over a high flame.

2
Add ½ teaspoon salt and the sliced cucumber. Boil for 1 minute.

3
Add the ground pork mixture and stir a few times. Bring to a boil again. Boil for 2 minutes.

4
Turn off the heat and add the cut scallion and pepper to taste. Let the soup sit for a few minutes; then serve.

JUST PLAIN SOUP

ingredients

1 scallion
1 tablespoon soy sauce
½ teaspoon peanut oil
½ teaspoon salt
3 cups water

Total prep & cooking time: 15 minutes

This soup doesn't taste like much. It should be served with a hot (spicy) dish to help wash away the hot taste. This simple soup will clear your palate so you can taste the other dishes better.

to prepare

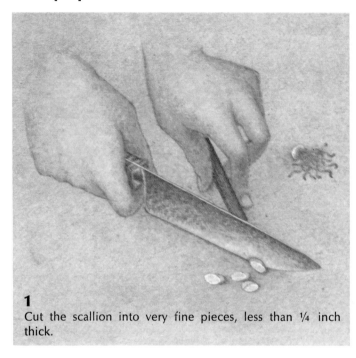

1
Cut the scallion into very fine pieces, less than ¼ inch thick.

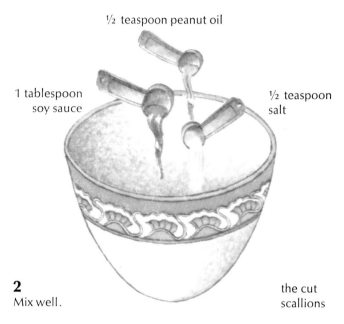

½ teaspoon peanut oil

1 tablespoon soy sauce

½ teaspoon salt

the cut scallions

2
Mix well.

to cook

1
Put 3 cups water into a saucepan. Turn flame to high and bring water to a boil.

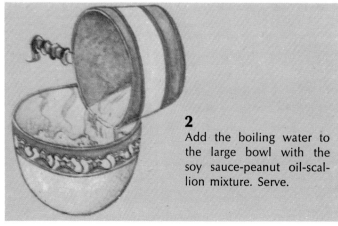

2
Add the boiling water to the large bowl with the soy sauce-peanut oil-scallion mixture. Serve.

EGG DROP SOUP

ingredients

1 egg
3 cups water
1 tablespoon soy sauce
1 teaspoon dry sherry
1 tablespoon cornstarch (about)

Total prep & cooking time: 10 minutes

to prepare

Break an egg into a bowl and beat it as for scrambled eggs.

to cook

1
Add 3 cups water to medium-size saucepan. Bring water to a boil over a high flame.

2
Add 1 tablespoon soy sauce and 1 teaspoon dry sherry to the boiling water.

3
Slowly pour the egg into the boiling water, stirring as you do so.

4
Add 1 tablespoon cornstarch, a little at a time, stirring continuously. Add enough cornstarch to make the soup look thick and slightly glossy. Serve.